50,000 DEGREES AND CLOUDY: A BETTER RESURRECTION

By Hollisa Alewine, PhD

DEDICATION

To Aunt Dean, Pete, and Danny. What we dream of, you know.

ACKNOWLEDGMENTS

Thanks to my proofreaders and editors, Carol Walker, Timothy Herron, and Lisa Runyon. They combed through the text with a short deadline, and for that they deserve much more than a line or two of acknowledgment. If I've allowed any errors to slip through, the oversight is mine, not theirs. I'm grateful for all the hard work the BEKY Book authors have put into writing and teaching books that build up instead of tear down. May we be granted the time and audience to write many more. To Staci, thank you for your tender loving care with these BEKY Books. I know you have a heart to serve the Father, and my prayer is that we'll bring comfort and hope to many with this book. To Lisa Rubel, you're always faithful to help us pick the right covers with your photographer's eye. Save me a piece of chocolate for our next big decision.

My husband Alan has always been extremely patient when I'm in the most active phase of writing, and he forgives my distraction and monosyllabic answers. Multiplied thanks to you for encouraging me and giving me space to work and grow in different directions as a writer. You were especially a rock in the deaths of my father, mother, and Aunt Dean, who was like a second mother. At our age, we realize that life is like being in the kitchen of a house with everyone we know when we're born. We're like all kinds of Legos. Little by little, our family and friends cross over to the "living room," and eventually, we realize the Legos have been reassembled there. We're still in the preparation room, and now we've become the missing pieces from the real living room. They're waiting for us, the final pieces; nevertheless, it's hard to let those pieces go first when they've fit so tightly and brightly into our lives and who we are.

There is much to appreciate in being able to visit Hebron, from Rabbi Eitan to those who offer the hospitality of refreshment for weary travelers. The place had a profound impact on me, and I still refer to the photographs to try to understand exactly what happened there. If we meet in person, ask me, but be prepared for a pretty hard-to-believe story.

Most of all, thanks to Adonai for the great gift of His ancient and immovable Word. He hid so many treasures of wisdom and understanding in plain sight, and He has to chuckle when His children discover them as if they are brand new. In that respect, His mercies are new every morning, and with the Father's help, we will merit to uncover more of that which only requires a heartfelt search of the Scriptures.

CONTENTS

GLOSSARY

Adonai – my Lord.

HaBrit HaChadasha – New Testament. In Hebrew, literally, "Renewed Covenant." The Hebrew word for new, chadash, also means renewed, as we apply the adjective to the New Moon. The moon is not new; it is the same moon. Its appearance is merely renewed each month. By the same token, Jeremiah 31:31 defines the terms of the New Covenant: the Torah will be written on the hearts of God's people. It is not a new Torah, but the old Torah renewed in a dynamic way because of the work of Yeshua, a better mediator than Moses.

Chag – Usually, a Biblical feast such as Passover, Shavuot, or Sukkot.

Chiastic/chiasm – A chiastic structure is a literary technique wherein a story is divided into two halves and the themes of the first half of the story are repeated in the second half of the story in reverse order. Furthermore, the two halves of the chiastic structure "point" to the most important element of the structure, the central axis. This is illustrated below, where "C" is the axis:

A. Daniel 2: Four Gentile world empires
      B. Daniel 3: Gentile persecution of Israel
           C. Daniel 4: Divine providence over Gentiles
           C'. Daniel 5: Divine providence over Gentiles
      B'. Daniel 6: Gentile persecution of Israel
A'. Daniel 7: Four Gentile world empires

Here is an example from the Book of Revelation by chapter, contributed by Mariela Perez-Rosas, with "G" as the axis:

A 1 Prologue and greeting: Alef-Tav[1]; He who comes
  B 2-3 Seven Assemblies
    C 4-5 Celestial Vision
      D 6-8 Seven Seals, Seven Trumpets
       E 7 The Sealed
        F 10-11 Angel, 2 Witnesses
         **G 12 The Woman -
         Male Son-
         Dragon**
        F 13 Dragon, 2 Beasts
       E 14 The New Song
      D 15-18 Seven Plagues, Seven Cups
    C 19-20 Celestial Vision
  B 21 New Jerusalem
A 22 Epilogue and farewell: Alef-Tav; He who comes

For an easy exercise in understanding chiastic structure, cut out the graphic of the menorah Appendix B. Fold the menorah along its axis, the middle branch of Weeks. The first and last branches will become "mirrors" of one another, as will the second and sixth branches and the third and fifth branches.

Elohim – God the Creator named in Genesis One

Erev Shabbat – the eve of Shabbat that starts at sundown on Friday evenings.

Gan Eden – The Garden of Eden, Paradise, or the Third Heaven

Hermeneutics – Methods of Biblical interpretation applying accepted rules of interpretation.

Ishim – a class of man-like angels who minister to human beings

1. Alpha and Omega in Greek.

Jubilee – The 50th year of the agricultural cycle in Israel marked by freedom of indentured servants and return of all ancestral properties.

Menorah – a lampstand, specifically, the seven-branched golden lampstand that stood in the Holy Place of the Tabernacle and Temple.

Mishnah – the Jewish oral law traditionally believed to have been passed down from Moses. Yeshua usually upheld the oral law of the House of Hillel, but he overruled most of the oral laws of the House of Shammai. They were the two predominant schools of the Pharisees in the First Century.

Metaphor – a thing regarded as representative or symbolic of something else, especially something abstract.

Mitzvah – commandment

Moed(im) - alludes to seasons and the appointed feasts of Israel: Passover, Unleavened Bread, Firstfruits of the Barley, Firstfruits of the Wheat (Pentecost), Trumpets, Day of Atonement, and Tabernacles

Nefesh – the bundle of appetites, desires, emotion, and intellect. It is vital energy that attaches to the body to preserve it.

Neshamah – the highest power of the *ruach* (spirit) of a man that bridges human and Divine realms. It is considered the holiest and most exalted part of a person.

Ruach HaKodesh – Holy Spirit, a level that joins the higher neshamah and nefesh, or animal-like soul.

Sukkah/sukkot – a covered booth or tabernacle

Talmud – the largest body of Jewish law and commentary containing the Mishnah, Gemara, and

Tosefta.

TANAKH – Old Testament. Tanakh is an acronym for Torah, Neviim, Ketuvim, or Law, Prophets, and Writings, the ancient divisions of the Hebrew Bible. The books of the Tanakh are the same as, but are not arranged in the same order as Christian Bibles.

Waqf – Muslim religious entity, funded by the King of Jordan, in control of the Temple Mount and other holy sites such as Hebron.

World to Come/Olam Haba - an enduring world after the Messianic reign created for people who are resurrected

Yeshua – Jesus' Hebrew name; salvation.

Yaval – a trumpet made from a ram's horn or sometimes the ibex horn

Yovel – see Jubilee

"It seems ridiculous to suppose the dead miss anything. If you're a grown man when you read this - it is my intention for this letter that you will read it then - I'll have been gone a long time. I'll know most of what there is to know about being dead, but I'll probably keep it to myself. That seems to be the way of things."

– Marilynne Robinson in *Gilead*

SECTION I

CLOUDS OF GLORY

1

WORDS IN THE 'HOOD

Many Christians believe in an end-time event called The Rapture. Since most believers also expect a time of worldwide catastrophe called The Tribulation, the timing of The Rapture is often intertwined with that event in both theological books and Christian fiction. For this reason, those who don't know evangelical Christian terminology find themselves confused when they hear the question, "Are you pre-trib, mid-trib, or post-trib?" One preacher humorously remarked, "I'm pan-trib. It'll all pan out in the end!"

Since the rapture can be controversial, this book offers an alternate method of viewing the event called The Rapture. A search of "the rapture" in a popular book database turned up over 6,000 items. With competition like that, a new book on The Rapture doesn't have much chance of edging the competition. For that reason, *50,000 Degrees and Cloudy* attempts something different. It starts at the beginning of the Bible. It consults the people-group that has been studying the Hebrew Scriptures for thousands of years.

The Rapture is based on some proof texts of New Testament, yet there is an older Scriptural basis for the expectation of a similar event, the resurrection of the dead. The understanding of the resurrection is based in the TANAKH, or the Old Testament. This view has been handed down faithfully to hundreds of generations of Jews, both those who believe in the Messiahship of Yeshua (Jesus), and those who do not. This would have been the common "ingathering" language and expectation of the Jewish populace in the First Century, including the apostles who penned the Christian proof texts.

Yeshua (Jesus) and the early apostles were Jewish, so it is logical to examine their expectation of end times. This is the due diligence of any Bible study, and it is one of the fundamental rules of hermeneutics taught both in Christian seminaries and Jewish yeshivot[2].

Some of the basics of biblical hermeneutics are:

- First Mention. The first appearance use of the word or phrase may hold a key to defining the word that will hold true through the Bible. The Torah, the first five books of the Bible, usually contains the First Mention of a word, phrase, or topic, so it becomes a Seed concept that leads to
- Progressive Mention. Progressive Mention is a process of chronicling each additional use of the word or phrase, studying it in its various contexts. This eventually leads to
- Complete Mention. When a complete study of the word or phrase's context is complete until the end of Scripture, it forms a full picture called Complete Mention. In addition, scholars agree that no verse of Scripture can yield a complete picture without taking into account its
- Historical context (history, geography, culture, religion, politics, etc.)

2. Similar to a Christian seminary; schools for learning Scripture and Jewish law based on the Scripture

Scholars agree that the one rule that summarizes them all is:

CONTEXT is everything!

There are other ways of describing how important context is, such as the Jewish idea of *smikhut* (placement). The real estate of the Biblical parchment is meaningful, so deriving meaning and significance depends upon location, location, location. Word, phrase, or concept repetition falls into the category of *smikhut*. In a book where there is only so much space to record Divine Words, the repetition of a word or phrase requires the reader to focus on the valuable placement in this prime "acreage" of the Bible. It also helps to check out the other "neighbors" in the neighborhood, which is other key words positioned closely or repeatedly in context.

An example is found in layering the themes of numbers in Scripture. For instance, the number three is generally accepted as representative of resurrection. If the number three is traced to its First Mention in the Creation week, then the pattern is established. The third day's creation was of trees and their "first fruits" to appear in the earth, just as Yeshua is called the "First Fruit from the Dead."[3] The Hebrew word for tree is *etz*. The Spirit of Counsel[4] is *etzah*, and it is the third (specific) Spirit of Adonai listed in Isaiah. What does good counsel do? It resurrects hope! The layers of 3s have a consistent theme.

A brief example of the First Mention seed concept of resurrection is found in the Third and Fifth Days of Creation. Count forward to the third light on the menorah above. The earth first yields living *plants* on the Third Day, which becomes a symbol of

3. 1 Co 15:20

4. Is 11:2

19

resurrection, or life springing forth from the earth. It is a day on which the chaotic waters are gathered so that the dry earth can emerge.

Figure 1

5. "And Jesus said to them, 'Follow Me, and I will make you become fishers of men.' Immediately they left their nets and followed Him." (Mk 1:17)

Now count three lights back from the end of the menorah. On the Fifth Day, the birds and fish are created, the first living *animals*. Hundreds of years later, a dove goes forth from the ark after the Flood, and she returns to Noah with a Third Day symbol of new life, an olive branch. Together, the plants, birds, and fish picture many examples of resurrection in Scripture. Yeshua first calls disciples[5] who will be "fishers of men" after his resurrection on the Third Day. Third Day trees and Fifth Day birds sometimes are paired as a symbol of resurrection:

6. Jewish tradition places the Palace of Messiah in the Lower Garden of Eden, and the palace is called kan ha-tzippor, or "the bird's nest."

> On the mountain height of Israel will I plant it, that it may bear branches and *produce fruit and become a noble cedar.* And under it will dwell *every kind of bird*; in the shade of its

branches *birds of every sort* will nest.[6]
And *all the trees of the field* shall
know that I am the Lord; I bring low
the high tree, and make high the
low tree, dry up the green tree, and
make the dry tree flourish. I am the
Lord; I have spoken, and I will do it.[7]

In Revelation, John prophesies that the sea will give up its dead and the earth will give up its dead to resurrection and judgment, symbolizing the resurrection of the Third Day "trees" and the Fifth Day "fish."

And the sea gave up the dead
which were in it, and death and
Hades gave up the dead which
were in them; and they were judged,
every one *of them* according to their
deeds[8].

Pairing birds and fish (Fifth Day of Creation) with sea or tree/plant themes (Third Day of Creation) in the same neighborhood links them textually as well as chiastically. A chiasm is a mirror-like structure with a written text or symbol. The Greek letter *chi* looks like the English letter *X*, which if folded on its axis in either direction, folds perfectly upon itself like a mirror image. The chiasm is used frequently in Scripture, helping the reader to find the center, essence, or theme that the passage explains.

Examine the drawing of the menorah[9] labeled with the Feasts of Israel in the preceding paragraphs. If the menorah is folded on its axis (fourth branch), then the Third and Fifth Days of Creation touch, for the third and fifth branches originate from the same spot on the central branch. A chiasm can also be written to demonstrate how each item is mirrored on the other side.

Here is an example from the Book of Daniel:

7. Ezek 17:23–24 ESV

8. Re 20:13

9. lampstand

A. Daniel 2: Four Gentile world empires
    B. Daniel 3: Gentile persecution of Israel
        C. Daniel 4: Divine providence over Gentiles
        C'. Daniel 5: Divine providence over Gentiles
    B'. Daniel 6: Gentile persecution of Israel
A'. Daniel 7: Four Gentile world empires

The word chiasm is based on the letter X, so the fold of the menorah can be made in both directions. The menorah represents the Seven Spirits of God in Scripture, and a rainbow has seven colors of covenant, also representing the Spiritual Light of the Word refracted into visible colors. Place the rainbow on top of the menorah, and the concentric circles form a full view of the Spirit as it may be seen from the earth or from Heaven above.

> As the appearance of *the rainbow in the clouds* on a rainy day, so was the appearance of the surrounding radiance. Such was the appearance of the likeness of the glory of the LORD.[10]

> And He who was sitting was like a jasper stone and a sardius in appearance; and there was *a rainbow around the throne*, like an emerald in appearance.[11]

This mirror-like depiction of Heaven and Earth reflects the description of the Garden of Eden in Genesis. A river flowed *out* of Eden and watered the whole Garden. This doesn't make sense, for if the river flowed *out*, then how could it water the whole Garden? Only if it is the River that flows out of the Heavenly Eden and waters the Lower Garden of Genesis.

10. Ezek 1:28

11. Re 4:3

> The LORD God planted a garden toward the east, in Eden; and there He placed the man whom He had

formed. Out of the ground the LORD
God caused to grow every tree that
is pleasing to the sight and good for
food; *the tree of life* also in the midst
of the garden, and the tree of the
knowledge of good and evil. Now a
river flowed *out* of Eden to water the
garden; and from there it divided
and became four rivers. The name
of the first is Pishon; it flows *around*
[sovev]...[12]

Then he showed me a river of the
water of life, clear as crystal, *coming
from the throne of God and of the
Lamb*, in the middle of its street. On
either side of the river was *the tree
of life*, bearing twelve kinds of fruit,
yielding its fruit every month; and
the leaves of the tree were for the
healing of the nations.[13]

Indeed, the description of the rivers around Eden
and the Tree of Life is better understood from the
Hebrew text, for it describes their movement as
circling, *sovev*, the Garden in the present tense. It
is still circling! As described in the Scripture above,
the appearance of the Spirit in Heaven is circling
the throne like a rainbow. A river flows from under
the Throne. Now the chiasm of the Lower Garden
and Upper Garden makes sense. This is important,
because the resting places of the Upper and Lower
Garden make up much of the understanding of what
happens to the righteous believer post-mortem.
Yeshua taught these things both in parables and in
very direct language, such as "this day you will be
with me in Paradise."[14] John also sees it in his vision:

He that hath an ear, let him hear
what the Spirit saith unto the
churches; To him that overcometh
will I give to eat of *the tree of life*,

12. Ge 2:8–11

13. Re 22:1–2

14. Lk 23:43

23

*which is in the midst of the paradise
of God.*[15]

While the curious Christian is most interested in "the rapture," the view is much wider, broader, and deeper than most explore. This investigation will cover a broad range of topics concerning death, burial, and resurrection, perhaps giving a better contextual view.

Here is one of the most common proof-texts for the rapture:

> For the Lord Himself will descend
> from heaven with a shout, with the
> voice of the archangel and with the
> trumpet of God, and the dead in
> Christ will rise first.
>
> Then we who are alive and remain
> will be caught up together with them
> in the clouds to meet the Lord in the
> air, and so we shall always be with
> the Lord.
>
> Therefore comfort one another with
> these words.[16]

Yeshua explained his resurrection to his disciples "beginning with Moses,"[17] the Torah,[18] so Yeshua's primary text is our primary text. Here are key New Covenant Seed words and concepts that are first located in the Torah:

- The Lord Himself **descends**.
- The dead **ascend**.
- The saints will **go up** with them.
- They meet the Lord **in the cloud together**.
- They **dwell** with the Lord forever.
- These words are **comfort**ing.

Since the keywords for rapture proof-texts are

15. Re 2:7 KJV

16. 1 Th 4:16–18

17. Lk 24:27

18. First five books of the Bible: Genesis, Exodus, Leviticus, Numbers, and Deuteronomy

"clouds" and going "up," then a good study looks at Seed texts from the Torah, additional texts from the rest of the TANAKH (Older Testament), as well as the Newer Testament (*Brit HaChadasha*). Additionally, even a brief study can apply the principle of historical context, which is the construction of Jewish expectation from these vital Scriptures. The seeds of the Word from the Torah will grow a full picture by the end of Revelation, a revelation of new life known as Clouds of Glory.

2

THE PHARISEES? ARE YOU KIDDING ME?

Most readers think "hypocrite" when they hear the word Pharisee or use it. Big mistake! Most Jewish lay people who lived in the First Century had an affection for the Pharisees, and Bible readers overlook facts about the Pharisees that are necessary to understanding Yeshua's interactions with them. The Pharisees prepared the Jews for a Messiah with their vital doctrine of resurrection of the dead, which put the Pharisees at odds with the Sadducees and gnostic cults.

All Pharisees were not hypocrites, and according to the truest *historical* definition of a Pharisee, most Christians would fall into that definition. Hypocrisy was added to the definition in *later* centuries. A very accurate historical quote sums up the First Century view of Pharisees:

> King Yannai said to his wife: 'Do not fear the Pharisees nor the non-Pharisees, but the hypocrites who *mimic* the Pharisees, because their deeds are the deeds of Zimri but they expect the reward of Pinchas.'[19]

19. Talmud Bavli Sotah 22b. For an easy reference to Jewish sources such as the Talmud, see S. Creeger's *Introduction to the Jewish Sources*, a BEKY Book.

Zimri fornicated in full view of the Tabernacle, but Pinchas took up a spear and killed him and his lover because he had zeal for the House of God.[20] Pharisees were zealous for God's Word. Christians would be surprised to find out how much they have in common with the righteous Pharisees, not the hypocrites whom Yeshua was obliged to correct and rebuke, those who mimicked the zeal of a Pharisee who loved the Word. For a simple, yet eye-opening explanation of the First Century Pharisees and how they were vital to Yeshua's ministry, see the BEKY Book, *Pharisee: Friend or Foe?* A few important points from the book are offered again here to establish the background of First Century epistles that mention resurrection.

The period of Greek ascension to world power likely birthed the more primitive sects that emerged into a group known as the Pharisees. Since the Pharisees are frequently assigned the role of pariah in the Gospels, it is useful to define the group and its historical origin. There were two main groups that comprise the larger group called Pharisee. Briefly, this defines the character of the Pharisaic groups:

Developed during the Maccabean Period from the "Hasidim" (pious ones). Several different groups like the Essenes came out of the anti-Hellenistic reaction to Antiochus IV Epiphanes and his cruel and immoral reign. Their major doctrines:

    A. Belief in a coming Messiah.
    B. God is active in daily life. This was directly opposite from the Sadducees. Much of Pharisaic doctrine is a theological counterpoint to the Sadducees' doctrines.
    C. A physically oriented afterlife based on earthly life, which involved reward and punishment.
    D. Authority of the OT and the Oral Traditions (*Talmud*).

20. Nu 25

28

E. Highly developed angelology. This involved
   both good and evil spiritual beings.[21]

Although Utley's description above is an academic
Bible reference, there is an anachronistic mistake in
"D." The Pharisees could not have believed in the
Talmud, for its earliest pages were not written until
two centuries after Messiah's death and resurrection,
and it was not finalized until the medieval period!
Such errors, though they seem small, are common
in Bible reference sources. These inaccuracies
make a significant impact. The Talmud represents
a vast quantity of *additional* commentary and
development from the Oral Traditions that existed
during the time that the Gospels were written.[22]

The Hebrew word for Pharisee is *Prushim or Prushin*.
Here is the Biblical context for the root word, *parash*.

> So they read in the book in the law
> of God distinctly (*parash*), and gave
> the sense, and caused *them* to
> understand the reading.[23]

> And they put him in custody, until
> the decision of the LORD should be
> made clear (*perosh*) to them.[24]

A Parush (Pharisee) was one who desired to give
distinct sense to the Hebrew Biblical text and to
disperse the knowledge so that the average person
could understand it and therefore obey it. For this
reason, the Pharisees had the hearts of the multitudes
of common people.

Most Bible students have a basic understanding of
Bible reference sources, how the Biblical canon was
decided, and who wrote or recorded its books and
letters. If the reference source is biased, however,
it can affect one's definition or perception of a
group of people from the outset. It is difficult to
correct a distorted first perception. For instance,

21. Utley, 2003,
pp. 86-87

22. For additional
examples,
see Dr. Robin
Gould's BEKY
Book *Colossal
Controversies*.

23. Ne 8:8

24. Le 24:12 NRSV

29

here is a Bible dictionary definition of a Pharisee that is available from a popular Bible software[25] application:

> Pharisee - a member of an ancient Jewish sect, distinguished by strict observance of the traditional and written law, and **commonly held to have pretensions to superior sanctity a self-righteous person; a hypocrite**. Old English *fariseus*, via ecclesiastical Latin from Greek *Pharisaios*, from Aramaic prīšayyā 'separated ones' (related to Hebrew pārūsh 'separated').

Nicely embedded within the scholarly description is a departure into stereotypes of how Pharisees came to be perceived in successive generations of Christian anti-Semitic polemics. Most people using a Bible dictionary already know what a Pharisee means *today*. Students of the Bible use a reference source, however, to find out what the word meant in its *original use* and context. If I am a new Bible student, then forever my first impression is that a Pharisee is and always was "commonly held to have pretensions to superior sanctity a self-righteous person; a hypocrite."

The logical conclusion for a student using the reference book is that "Pharisees are hypocrites." Although dictionaries are usually credible sources, the Bible student is not served well with this entry. Perhaps another reliable source, such as Strong's, will do better. *Strong's*[26] definition of a Pharisee is even more damning:

> A sect that started after the Jewish exile. In addition to OT books the Pharisees recognised in oral tradition a standard of belief and life. They sought for distinction and praise by

25. LOGOS

26. Retrieved 9/3/18 from https://www. blueletterbible. org/lang/ lexicon/lexicon. cfm?Strongs G5330&t=NKJV

outward observance of external rites and by outward forms of piety, and such as ceremonial washings, fastings, prayers, and alms giving; and, comparatively negligent of genuine piety, they prided themselves on their fancied good works. They held strenuously to a belief in the existence of good and evil angels, and to the expectation of a Messiah; and they cherished the hope that the dead, after a preliminary experience either of reward or of penalty in Hades, would be recalled to life by him, and be requited each according to his individual deeds. In opposition to the usurped dominion of the Herods and the rule of the Romans, they stoutly upheld the theocracy and their country's cause, and possessed great influence with the common people. **They were bitter enemies of Jesus and his cause; and were in turn severely rebuked by him for their avarice, ambition, hollow reliance on outward works, and affection of piety in order to gain popularity.**

This dictionary says that Pharisees were arch-enemies of Jesus, full of pride, greedy, prioritizing rituals over spiritual change, and popularity-seekers! It's not looking good for the Pharisees, but neither is it looking good for the new Bible student who will miss vital lessons that the Gospels, Acts, and even Revelation teach about the Pharisees and their doctrine of resurrection. In fact, almost obscured by the stereotypical characteristics is the *accurate* information the student truly needs:

> They held strenuously to a belief
> in the existence of good and evil

angels, and to the expectation
of a Messiah; and they cherished
the hope that the dead, after a
preliminary experience either of
reward or of penalty in Hades,
would be recalled to life by him
[resurrection], and be requited each
according to his individual deeds.

Presented with two kinds of information about the Pharisees, that which is analytical and that which is filtered through stereotype, many unsuspecting readers will adopt the stereotype; after all, it does make for juicy reading! The problem with both dictionaries, though, is the omitted defining texts about the Pharisees from *all* the contexts, both written and historical. The Bible records some wonderful things about individual Pharisees, and the very coming of Messiah was to a stage prepared by the Pharisees' fundamental doctrines.

These dictionaries' definitions encase the real meat of Pharisaic faith between two large pieces of stereotypical bread, forcing the naïve reader into a dilemma. Either she must picture the Pharisees as greedy, ritualistic, proud haters of Jesus, or conclude that Pharisees preached the coming of Messiah and the resurrection of the dead. The fact that both dictionaries' definitions include the modern pejorative use of Pharisee is troubling.

The problem goes beyond stereotypes. The definitions lure the reader into a logical fallacy, which is a form of mind manipulation. This particular fallacy is commonly called The Hasty Generalization. A Hasty Generalization draws a general rule from atypical cases.

Example:

(1) My Christian neighbor tells off-color jokes.

Therefore:

(2) Christians tell off-color jokes.

This argument takes an individual case of a Christian and draws a general rule from it, assuming that all Christians are like the atypical neighbor. The conclusion is foolish because it doesn't demonstrate a common characteristic of all Christians. It may be that the neighbor is not a typical Christian, so the conclusion is false. Maybe he goes to church because it's a way of establishing business contacts. The truth is that many more neighbors may come forward who have never heard their Christian neighbors tell off-color jokes.

It is important to have a good definition of a Pharisee, for they played a fundamental role in First Century Messianic expectation and the spread of the gospel.

What many students do not know are basic historical facts that affect one's reading of the text, especially in a translation such as English. For instance, Lk 16:13-15 in the *New American Standard Bible* reads thus:

No servant can serve two masters; for either he will hate the one and love the other, or else he will be devoted to one and despise the other. You cannot serve God and weath.

↓   ↓

Now the Pharisees, who were lovers of money, were listening to all these things and were scoffing at Him.

And He said to them, 'You are those who justify yourselves in the sight of men, but God knows your hearts; for that which is highly esteemed among men is detestable in the sight of God.' (Lk 16:13-15)

The appositive phrase, "who were lovers of money," is enclosed with commas. The English translator's grammar doesn't just imply, but states, that all the Pharisees were lovers of money. Is this the best place for commas?

New Testament Greek, like the Hebrew of the TANAKH, was not written with punctuation or capital letters. For instance, here is an example of a TANAKH Hebrew text, followed by an example of Greek text:

Figure 2

CKΛICIΛΘΝΔΙΟΤΙΕΕΝΓΗCEΔΡΑΧKΛIΔ
ΛΗΜΜΔΛΟΓΟΥ iC·KΛICIΛΘΝΔΙΟΤΙΕ
ΕΝΓΗCEΔΡΑΧKΛIΔΦΡΟΡΗCΑCΦΟΔΡΧ
ΑΜΑCKΟYΘYCIΛΛYKΛIω·KΟΔΟΜΗCΕΝ
ΤΟΥ TIKCEΦΡΑΤYΡΟCΟΧYΡωΜΑ
ΑΝΘΡωΠΟΥCKΠΑCΤΑΔΥΤΗCKΛIΕΘΗ
ΑCΦΥΛΑCΤΟYIΗΧCΑYΡICΕΝΑΡΓΥΡΕ
KΛIΕΝΕΜΑΘΕΤΟICIΟΝωCΧΟYKΔIΧΡΥ
ΟΡIΟICΑYΤΗCΤYΡΟΛΗΜΜΔΛΟΓΟΥ
CKΛICIΔΘΝΔΙΟΤΙΕΕΝΓΗCEΔΡΑΧKΛIΔ
ΦΡΟΡΗCΑCΦΟΔΡΑΑΜΑCKΟYΘYCIΛΛY
KΛIωKΟΔΟΜΗCΕΝΤΟΥ TIKCEΦΡΑ
ΤYΡΟCΟΧYΡωΜΑΑΝΘΡωΠΟΥCKΠΑC
ΤΑΔΥΤΗCKΛIΕΘΗΑCΦΥΛΑCΤΟYIΗΧ
CΑYΡICΕΝΑΡΓΥΡΕKΛIΕΝΕΜΑΘΕΤΟIC
IΟΝωCΧΟYKΔIΧΡΥΟΡIΟICΑYΤΗCΤYΡΟ
ΛΗΜΜΔΛΟΓΟΥ iCKΛICIΔΘΝΔΙΟΤΙΕ
ΕΝΓΗCEΔΡΑΧKΛIΔΦΡΟΡΗCΑCΦΟΔΡΑ
ΑΜΑCKΟYΘYCIΛΛYKΛIωKΟΔΟΜΗCΕΝ
ΤΟΥ TIKCEΦΡΑΤYΡΟCΟΧYΡωΜΑ
ΑΝΘΡωΠΟΥCKΠΑCΤΑΔΥΤΗCKΛIΕΘΗ
ΑCΦΥΛΑCΤΟYIΗΧCΑYΡICΕΝΑΡΓΥΡΕ
KΛIΕΝΕΜΑΘΕΤΟICIΟΝωCΧΟYKΔIΧΡΥ
ΟΡIΟICΑYΤΗCΤYΡΟΛΗΜΜΔΛΟΓΟΥ

Figure 3

No punctuation or capital letters there! The New Testament letters were usually delivered by people who knew the writer's intent and explained or taught it, such as Phoebe for Paul's letter to the Romans. It ensured that the lack of punctuation did not result in misunderstanding.

What if the sentence is re-written without the translator's commas?

> Now the Pharisees who were lovers of money were listening to all these things and were scoffing at Him.

With this punctuation, the reader is not tempted to paint all Pharisees as money-lovers with a broad brush. Among those Pharisees who were listening, those who *did* love money began to scoff at him. In any church, there is a usually a subgroup who may attend faithfully, yet they are there only for business contacts or to be seen "doing the right thing" in order to maintain community standing. Why would we expect Pharisees to be different than any other religious denomination? Even more examples of how the Pharisees themselves viewed hypocrites and stingy people are given in *Pharisee: Friend or Foe?*

While most Bible students would not automatically categorize a rich person as evil, it would be easy to use the same stereotype as is used with the Pharisees. There are a few instances in Scripture where it speaks of the rich as evil, such as:

> Is it not the rich who oppress you and
> personally drag you into court? Do
> they not blaspheme the fair name
> by which you have been called?[27]

If we take out of context this or Yeshua's caution about it being difficult for a rich man to enter the Kingdom of Heaven, then it may appear that *all*

27. Ja 2:6-7

rich men are evil blasphemers who oppress poor people. The full context of Scripture, however, has examples of generous righteous rich men and women, such as Job, Abraham, the Queen of Sheba, Lydia, Joseph of Arimathea, or the high-ranking[28] Pharisee[29] Nicodemus, who did not consent to Yeshua's death[30] in the "kangaroo court" assembled by the Sadducees:

> When it was evening, there came
> a rich man from Arimathea, named
> Joseph, who himself had also
> become a disciple of Jesus. This man
> went to Pilate and asked for the
> body of Jesus. Then Pilate ordered it
> to be given to him. And Joseph took
> the body and wrapped it in a clean
> linen cloth, and laid it in his own new
> tomb...[31]

> Nicodemus, who had first come to
> Him by night, also came, bringing a
> mixture of myrrh and aloes, about a
> hundred pounds weight.[32]

Stereotyping certainly removes a lot of the burden to diligently study the Scriptures, but taking full context is a challenge and hard work. It requires putting together not just the simple meaning of the text, but what it meant to the people who spoke the words. To the Pharisee of the First Century, a truly and spiritually rich person was "the one who is satisfied with what he has..."[33]

Alternatively, another type of rich person was spiritually deficient, greedy, and had a grander view of himself than any honorable Pharisee should have. This type of rich person is not just found lurking among the First Century Pharisees; he is lurking among the end-time Seven Assemblies of Revelation:

> So because you are lukewarm, and

28. Mk 15:43

29. Jn 3:1

30. Lk 23:51

31. Mt 27:57-60

32. Jn 19:39

33. Avot 4:1

neither hot nor cold, I will spit you
out of My mouth. Because you say, 'I
am rich, and have become wealthy,
and have need of nothing,' and you
do not know that you are wretched
and miserable and poor and blind
and naked...[34]

The language in Revelation is reminiscent of the
quotation from *Pirkei Avot*. The spiritually rich person
is satisfied with the earthly goods that he has. This
makes him truly "have need of nothing," for he trusts
Adonai to meet his needs. The obverse is true. Those
who are satisfied that they are already sufficient
in spiritual goods will find that they are very poor,
and in fact, they need much more to be rich in the
Kingdom! Like Yeshua said, they look good on the
outside with acts of piety, but the inside is a grave of
the spirit.

Another example of English word selection is in the
following verse:

And when he was **demanded**
[*eperotao*] **of the Pharisees**, when
the kingdom of God should come,
he answered them and said, 'The
kingdom of God cometh not with
observation...'[35]

The Greek word (G1905) *eperotao* is translated as
"demand." The verb is from G1909 and G2065,
which mean:

to ask for, i.e. inquire, seek: ask
(after, questions), demand, desire,
question.

The translation of "demanded" is most puzzling,
for how many times is that particular Greek word
translated as the more innocuous "asked" instead of
the emotionally-charged "demanded"? For English-

34. Re 3:16-17

35. Lk 17:20 KJV

37

speakers, there is a marked visceral difference in the reaction to someone who asks or inquires versus someone who demands.

The KJV translates Strong's G1905 with the following English words:

ask (53x) ◀
demand (2x)
desire (1x)
ask question (1x)
question (1x)
ask after (1x)

Although the translators select "ask" 53 times in other contexts, in relation to the Pharisees, they select "demand," one of only two times the word is translated with such negativity! This does not mean that the English Bible is chock-full of poor word selections. It means that study tools are freely available when a reader sees that something just doesn't add up.

The Pharisees were not as prevalent[36] as Bible readers would think, but one could expect they were over-represented as a group in the gospels because they were active in the sphere of religious activity. They would have been especially interested in another reformist who was preaching many of their doctrines and who was popular in the Galilee.

The Gospels highlight the Pharisees because their history was so connected doctrinally to Yeshua, and their paths frequently intersected, for they shared audiences. Since Yeshua's very life, death, and resurrection was a validation of the Pharisees' teaching, we might even say that the Pharisees prepared the stage for Yeshua's arrival in his particular generation. His preaching of resurrection fell on many Jewish ears prepared to hear. His Messianic works were believed by many Jewish eyes

36. This is based on their sparse mention in Josephus' historical works, although he was also a Pharisee for a period.

prepared to see.

In reality, though, the Pharisees were a small number of people. It was their doctrine of *resurrection* that brings them into Biblical focus, not their large numbers. The number of Pharisees at the time of Herod may have been around 6,000.[37] Various sources report that 3,000,000 – 4,000,000 Jews and converts filled Jerusalem during annual feasts, so the ratio of Pharisees to total population is very small.

The small number of Pharisees relative to the general population of First Century Jews tells the reader that their great impact both in the hearts of the common people and in the gospels was vital to the presentation of Yeshua's message. Yeshua arrived as the embodiment of what the Pharisees taught.

For instance, Yeshua affirms the Pharisaic doctrine of eternal reward and punishment:

> Let the one who does wrong, still
> do wrong; and the one who is filthy,
> still be filthy; and let the one who is
> righteous, still practice righteousness;
> and the one who is holy, still keep
> himself holy. Behold, I am coming
> quickly, and *My reward is with Me,*
> *to render to every man according*
> *to what he has done.* I am the
> Alpha and the Omega, the first
> and the last, the beginning and the
> end. Blessed are those who wash
> their robes, so that they may have
> the right to the *tree of life*, and
> may enter by the gates into the
> city. *Outside* are the dogs and the
> sorcerers and the immoral persons
> and the murderers and the idolaters,
> and everyone who loves and
> practices lying.[38]

37. Saldarini, 2001, p. 99

38. Re 22:10-15

There are other examples of Yeshua's and Paul's identification with Pharisaic interpretation:

- Mark 12:18-27 & Matthew 22:23-33. Sadducees challenge Yeshua on resurrection, the essence of his mission. Yeshua cites Exodus 3:6 and says, "He is God, not of the dead, but of the living; you are quite wrong." To Yeshua, the Torah taught resurrection, a doctrine of the Pharisees.
- In Acts 23:6-7, the Apostle Paul declares: "I am a Pharisee, a son of Pharisees; I am on trial concerning the hope of the resurrection of the dead."

Yeshua's central message of forgiveness of sin and resurrection of the dead was not unusual or objectionable to the Pharisees or their adherents. "A central belief in their [the Pharisees'] reading of Judaism is a composite doctrine of the afterlife which includes both bodily resurrection and spiritual immortality."[39] This doctrine was in dispute among First Century Jews. It was rejected by Sadducees who controlled the Temple, and therefore they greatly controlled Jewish tax money. Disbelief in resurrection had economic tentacles attached to Rome. Other sects rejected a bodily resurrection, opting for a disembodied spiritual existence.

Yeshua clears up the question in his post-resurrection appearance to the disciples:

> But they were startled and frightened and thought that they were seeing a spirit. And He said to them, 'Why are you troubled, and why do doubts arise in your hearts? See My hands and My feet, that it is I Myself; touch Me and see, for a spirit does not have flesh and bones as you see that I have.' And when

39. Gillman, 2015, p. 121

He had said this, He showed them His hands and His feet. While they still could not believe it because of their joy and amazement, He said to them, 'Have you anything here to eat?' They gave Him a piece of a broiled fish; and He took it and ate it before them.[40]

Yeshua overturns the eschatological doctrines of the Essenes and Sadducees. He affirms the faith of the Pharisees.

The Pharisees also believed in the Holy Spirit and its role in the resurrection of the dead:

> Rabbi Pinhas ben Yair said: Torah leads to vigilance; vigilance leads to alacrity; alacrity leads to blamelessness, blamelessness leads to separateness from the worldly; separateness leads to purity; purity leads to piety; piety leads to humility; humility leads to fear of sin; fear of sin leads to sanctity; sanctity leads to the holy spirit; *the holy spirit leads to resurrection*.[41]

From a Jewish, and likely a Pharisaic standpoint, the gift of the Holy Spirit leads to resurrection from the dead. When Yeshua commands his disciples to remain in Jerusalem until the Feast of Shavuot (Pentecost), he extends this Pharisaic understanding to the nations. The Holy Spirit given to the Gentile converts in Acts Two proved that they also can receive the gift of resurrection from the dead, the essence of Pharisee Paul's mission to the Gentiles.

The Pharisees had neither horns nor halos. They were just people. Some were sincere, others insincere, and probably many were in-between, just like most religious groups. People look for religious leaders

40. Lk 24:37-43

41. Luzatto, 2007, p. 43

who are examples and who live according to the most ideal expression of the faith. The fact that Yeshua called out the greedy and hypocritical individuals validates the existence of the pious ones like Nicodemus. Thanks to the Pharisees and their successors in the rabbinic period who recorded their doctrines, the way was prepared for Yeshua, the Messiah who came preaching resurrection from the dead, reward and punishment, the Holy Spirit, and the involvement of angels in the world.

3

"RAPTURE" TEXTS IN JEWISH TRADITION

There are some texts that Christians commonly associate with the Rapture. One of those texts is in Paul's letter to the Thessalonians. Presumably the assembly at Thessalonica was primarily Gentile, so they were uninformed about Jewish tradition concerning the resurrection of the dead. This text, which concerns the greater resurrection,[42] instructs this assembly in Jewish thought.

> But we do not want you to be uninformed, brethren, about those who are asleep, so that you will not grieve as do the rest who have no hope. For if we believe that Jesus died and rose again, even so God will bring with Him those who have fallen asleep in Jesus.
>
> For this we say to you by the word of the Lord, that we who are alive and remain until the coming of the Lord, will not precede those who have fallen asleep.[43]

42. A first resurrection occurred during Passover week when Yeshua resurrected along with the saints of old, who were seen walking through the streets of the Holy City.

43. 1 Th 4:13–15

44. *Rosh HaShanah* means "head of the year." For a discussion about potential conflicts between the first of the months occurring in the spring and the head of the year occurring in the fall, see *Truth, Tradition, or Tare: Growing in the Word* by the author.

45. The Biblical year is not calculated like the secular year, which is solar and rooted in Roman history. The Biblical year takes into account the monthly lunar phases as well as solar seasons. For an explanation of the Biblical lunar calendar, see BEKY Book, *The Biblical New Moon*, by Kisha Gallagher.

46. See *Creation Gospel Workbook Three: The Spirit-filled Family* for a more thorough discussion of the male/female mirrors in Scripture.

This is a reference to the Biblical Feast of Trumpets (*Yom Teruah*), a feast day in Jewish tradition known as *Rosh HaShanah*.[44] Rosh HaShanah, or the Feast of Trumpets, in Jewish tradition is a resurrection day. The year ages,[45] dies, and those who walk with the Holy One are figuratively resurrected as newborns to a new year of obstacles to overcome on Rosh HaShanah. Sleeping is figurative of death, just as Adam and Abraham were put into a deep sleep before they were awakened to mirror "doubles" of covenant relationship, male and female.[46]

> The fact that we awake from sleep is some evidence for the resurrection. - *Genesis Rabba* 78.

Shouting, the trumpet, kingship over the whole earth, and resurrection are all Jewish themes associated with Rosh HaShanah. They are grown from the Seed of the Torah, the Psalms and Prophets. For instance, Psalm 47 is a song about the fall feasts of Israel, specifically the Feast of Trumpets, Rosh HaShanah:

> O **clap your hands**[47], all peoples; **shout** to God with the voice of joy. For the Lord Most High is to be feared, a great **King over all the earth**. He subdues peoples under us and **nations** under our feet. He chooses our inheritance for us, the glory of Jacob whom He loves. Selah.
>
> **God has ascended with a shout**, the Lord, **with the sound of a trumpet**. Sing praises to God, sing praises; sing praises to our **King**, sing praises. For God is the **King** of all the earth; sing praises with a skillful psalm. God reigns over the **nations**, God sits on His **holy throne**. The princes of the

people have assembled themselves
as the people of the God of
Abraham, for the shields of the earth
belong to God; He is highly exalted.

Inspired from this and other passages of the TANAKH[48], the Jewish liturgy in a *machzor*[49] contains scores of words and phrases with themes of royal kingship, the throne, shouting, ruling the nations, blowing the trumpets and shofars,[50] and resurrection of the "sleepers." A most famous hymn sung at Rosh HaShanah is "Our Father, Our King." These prayers are offered at the fall feast of Rosh HaShanah, the Feast of Trumpets.

The puzzle is how the Israelites came to connect a very short, cryptic commandment to observe a "Day of Blowing" with all these seasonal themes:

- Resurrection
- Shouting
- Blowing a shofar as well as trumpets
- A beginning of the year
- Royalty and the Throne of God
- Ruling the Nations
- Clouds
- White garments
- Judgment
- Repentance
- Remembrance

Can you see the themes above connected to this very short text?

> Also in the day of your gladness and in your appointed feasts, and on the first *days* of your months, you shall blow the trumpets over your burnt offerings, and over the sacrifices of your peace offerings; and they shall be as a reminder of you before your God. I am the Lord your God.[51]

47. The Hebrew word for "clap" can also be translated as "blow" (the trumpet).

48. Old Testament

49. Jewish prayerbook holding the services of prayer for the High Holy Days of Rosh HaShanah.

50. Trumpets formed from ram's horns or the long horns of the ibex.

51. Nu 10:10

It is difficult to see all those themes! The clue, however, is found in the neighborhood, a principle of *smikhut*, or word placement. Adjacent words or phrases can give the reader additional insight. In what appears to be a change of topic in the succeeding verses is the clue:

> Now in the second year, in the second month, on the twentieth of the month, **the cloud was lifted** from over the tabernacle of the testimony; and **the sons of Israel set out** on their journeys from the wilderness of Sinai. **Then the cloud settled down** in the wilderness of Paran. **So they moved out for the first time according to the commandment of the Lord through Moses.**[52]

The clue is movement in the cloud.

According to Jewish tradition, there was more than one aspect to the cloud. Yes, there was a pillar of cloud by day, but they also teach that Israel entered into the "Clouds of Glory" or "Tabernacles of Glory" when they traveled from Rameses to Sukkot in the Exodus. There the Holy One covered the nation with a habitation of cloud that protected them from serpents and scorpions below, enemies on every side, and the heat of the sun by day:

> Thus they set out from the mount of the LORD three days' journey, with the ark of the covenant of the LORD journeying in front of them for the three days, to seek out a resting place for them. *The cloud of the LORD was over them* by day when they set out from the camp.[53]

52. Nu 10:11-13

53. Nu 10:33-34

46

The manna fell, and the "tree" and "rock" gave them water in the wilderness. The Hebrew word for Egypt is Mitzraim, which can translate as "from the tribulations." Within the cloud, the Israelites constructed a Tabernacle so that the Divine Presence could "dwell among them" (Israel):

> And there I will meet with the
> children of Israel, *and the tabernacle*
> *shall be sanctified by my glory*....and
> they shall know that I am the LORD
> their God, that brought them forth
> out of the land of Egypt, that I may
> dwell among *them*: I am the LORD
> their God.[54]

The Tabernacle was the focal point of worship to bring the nation into unity; within that cloud of national unity, the Divine Presence could dwell, just as Paul wrote to the Thessalonians, "...so shall we ever be with the Lord." Now John's verses and Paul's letters make more sense:

> These are *the ones who come out*
> *of the great tribulation*, and they
> have washed their robes and made
> them white in the blood of the Lamb.
> For this reason, they are before
> the throne of God; and they serve
> Him day and night in His temple;
> and *He who sits on the throne will*
> *spread His tabernacle over them.*
> *They will hunger no longer, nor thirst*
> *anymore; nor will the sun beat down*
> *on them, nor any heat*; for the Lamb
> in the center of the throne will be
> their shepherd, and will guide them
> to springs of the water of life; and
> God will wipe every tear from their
> eyes."[55]

The "booths" described in the Feast of Tabernacles[56]

54. Ex 29:43, 46

55. Re 7:14-17

56. Please refer to S. Creeger's *Growing in Holiness: the Hebrew Calendar Day by Day* for more information on the feasts, particularly the Feast of Tabernacles.

are *sukkot* in Hebrew. These sukkot of glory, or clouds of glory, are the destination of Israel at the resurrection. It is there that Israel dwells in the Presence of the Divine Glory with Yeshua forever.

4

GOING UP OR SETTLING DOWN?

Although the Torah's wilderness narrative is challenging, it is this very narrative that seeds Jewish thought concerning the resurrection of the dead at Rosh HaShanah. The Angel of the Presence, who appears as a revelation of Yeshua to lead the Israelites, is at the forefront of their movements. This Angel who dwells in a cloud by day and fire by night gathers and moves the camp of Israel, which is signaled by the blowing of trumpets. Being in the cloud with the Angel of the Presence is a reference to Israel's wilderness walk after being redeemed from Egypt, when they dwelled under the cloud.

According to Jewish tradition, the Israelites entered the cloud during the Passover week on their first stop after they left Egypt, a location called Sukkot. The *Targum Onkelos* [57] records how Leviticus 23:42-44 was interpreted by the ancient Jewish sages:

> Live in booths seven days. Every citizen in Israel must live in booths, *so that future generations will know that I made the people of Israel dwell in the shade* [58] *of My cloud when I took them from the land of Egypt. I the Lord am your God. Moses spoke*

57. Drazin, 1994, p. 210

58. Some versions of the Targums have "shades of My clouds" instead of shade, singular.

49

about the order of the set times of the Lord, and he taught them to the Israelites.

In other fragments of the ancient Targums, the protective cover of the cloud is mentioned as the shade of glory,[59] and in agreement with the Cairo Geniza Targum Fragments, the *Targum to the Pentateuch*, Codex Vatican, Neofitti I states:

"...so that future generations will know that the clouds of the glory of My Shekinah, which were like booths..."

Another source describes the sukkot of glory similarly:

...the sukkot of the verse refer to the clouds of glory that accompanied the Israelites in the desert...what are the clouds of glory...according to the tradition, these clouds not only led the way but also leveled the path by removing steep hills and valleys. One tradition states that there were seven clouds-one on each of the four sides, one above to protect the Israelites from the rain and sun, one below to kill scorpions, and the seventh to lead the way and level the ground. Most of all, the cloud was a sign representing God's presence, or was even His actual presence, for it says: 'The cloud covered the Tent of Meeting, and the Presence of the Lord filled the Tabernacle. Moses could not enter the Tent of Meeting, because the cloud had settled upon it and the Presence of the Lord filled the Tabernacle.'[60]

59. *Targum Pseudo-Jonathan; Targum Onkelos,* and Sperber, 1959.

60. Strassfeld, 1985, p. 142

The last words of Leviticus Chapter Twenty-three above were not separated from the words of Chapter Twenty-four in the ancient text. Chapters and verses were inserted much later. The summary of the set times of Israel is connected thematically to the lighting of the golden menorah.

The Lord spoke with Moses, saying:

> Command the Israelites to bring
> to you clear olive oil, beaten, for
> lightning, to light the [menorah] lights
> forever...*this is a perpetual law for all
> generations.*[61]

In *Creation Gospel Workbook One*, the link between the Seven Churches of Revelation and the Seven Feasts of Israel is established by Scripture texts and Jewish tradition.[62] Additionally, the Lamp before the Throne is explained to the reader as serving a dual symbolic role: The Seven Churches *and* the Seven Spirits of God before the Throne. As metaphors reiterating the apocalyptic importance of the Seven Feasts, the text of Leviticus is reaffirmed, for readers were to understand that the set times were of importance to "future generations" and that the link to the menorah was a "perpetual law for all generations."

Other Targums succinctly explain what it means to be under the "Cloud of Glory": "so that future generations will know that the clouds of the glory of My Shekinah, which were like booths..."[63] The Presence of Adonai inhabits the nation of Israel as Israel inhabits the Cloud. The metaphor of Sukkot both as the first stop upon Israel's exit from Egypt and a cloud of Divine Presence is the accepted translation of the Exodus 13:20 text.

The cloud-dwelling is called "Sukkot of Glory." The first Biblical feast, Passover, is therefore connected with the last feast, Sukkot. The Creator declares

61. *Targum
Onkelos* to
Leviticus 24:2

62. See
Appendix A

63. Darzin, 2000,
p. 210

the end from the beginning! In a beautiful picture of the wholeness, completeness, and unity of the one Holy Spirit, which is characterized by the seven manifestations of that Holy Spirit listed in Isaiah 11, the seven feasts of Israel are represented by entering into the last feast, Sukkot, during the first feast, Passover.

Now one can appreciate why Paul assumed that these reminders of the fall and spring feasts, Passover and Sukkot, would comfort his readers. Paul even describes the gathering of the saints into the clouds (*nephele*), not cloud, which is consistent with the rabbinic interpretations. The Greek word *nephele*, or clouds, is identified in Biblical usage as "the cloud which led the Israelites in the wilderness."[64] The cloud is both singular and plural in theme, for it is the habitation of many individuals, yet it is one protective cloud.

The First Mention context of a moving cloud in which to dwell with the Presence of God was written from ancient times to Israel: "...the cloud was lifted from over the *tabernacle* of the testimony; and the sons of Israel set out on their journeys...then the cloud settled down... So they moved out *for the first time according to the commandment of the Lord through Moses*."[65]

Since Paul assures the Thessalonians that what he is writing is "by the Word of the Lord," we are left to wonder to where in the Word he is referring? Sukkot, which is also known as the Feast of Tabernacles, or the Feast of the Nations, begins in the fall with the Feast of Trumpets, Rosh HaShanah. Paul knew that Jewish readers would have context, but those unfamiliar with the Word[66] of the Lord would need solid clues to understand how they would go up at the resurrection of the dead.

The Seeds of resurrection are sown in the Torah, notably on every day of Creation, but let's focus on Day Five of Creation. On Day Five, the Creator made the covered, feathered birds to go up in swarms and

64. Thayer's Greek Lexicon

65. Ex 10:11-13

66. For a full discussion of the Torah as the Word (as well as the rest of the Scriptures all the way to Revelation), see BEKY Book *What is the Torah?*

the fish to swarm down. This is a chiastic mirror as mentioned in the Introduction, but the Hebrew root of the words translated as "swarm" or "swarming" is *ratz*. The root word suggests huge numbers of rapidly moving feet!

This up-swarm describes the resurrection of the dead as those multitudes who are already asleep in both land and sea being "given up,"[67] as well as those who are alive and remain to go up into the cloud. Was Yeshua making a tongue-in-cheek statement when he told his disciples to shake the dust of their feet from the communities who did not receive their message? If they rejected the Word of the Lord, they were dead in the dust already!

There are resurrection clues throughout the first five books of the Bible, but the most specific clues in the Word of the Lord are in the traditional Jewish Torah portions *Behaalotkha*, *Ki Tisa* and *Pekudei*. Jews re-read the Torah each year according to an assigned cycle, and each weekly portion has a name based on its beginning words. Put the names of these three reading portions together, and they say,

> "In your going up, when you elevate, at the reckoning."

From those Torah portions come most Jewish traditions of Rosh HaShanah (Feast of Trumpets).

> Behaalotkha "in your going up" (to light the menorah)[68] is in Numbers 8:1-12:16
>
> Ki Tisa "when you elevate" is in Numbers 30:11-34:35
>
> Pekudei "accounting, reckoning" is in Numbers 38:21-40:38

67. Re 20:13

68. Nu 8:1-12:6; 30:11-34:35; 38:21-40:38

Elevation and reckoning are the seasonal expectation of Rosh HaShanah, Yom HaKippurim, and Sukkot in ancient Jewish literature such as the Mishnah: "all the world passes under the Shepherd's staff" for judgment.

> Now as to *the times and the epochs*, brethren, you have no need of anything to be written to you. For you yourselves know full well that *the day of the Lord* will come *just like a thief in the night*. While they are saying, "Peace and safety!" then destruction will come upon them suddenly *like labor pains upon a woman with child*, and they will not escape. But you, brethren, are not in darkness, that *the day* would overtake you like a thief; for you are all sons of light and sons of day. We are not of night nor of darkness.[69]

The Day is Rosh HaShanah. On that day, the Last Trump (shofar) blows to call the elect from the four winds at the resurrection. Ten days later is Yom Kippur. Yom HaKippurim is the exact title of the feast. Yom HaKippurim is also a day, yet it is begun on Rosh HaShanah ten days earlier. The decrees of Rosh HaShanah are sealed up in the books at the conclusion of Yom HaKippurim. Without purporting to establish more than is stated in Scripture, what is implied is based on the Jewish tradition of three general classes of people:

a) completely righteous: people resurrected into the cloud on "the Day," Rosh HaShanah
b) intermediates; people whom Yeshua calls calls "lukewarm;"[70] they have ten days to repent before their destruction is sealed
c) completely wicked: people who neither desire to repent, nor to experience salvation

69. 1 Th 5:1–5

70. Re 3:16

54

Believers in Paul's day were well-versed in the Torah and Prophets, for it was the Bible that they used. All would have been familiar with the Seven Feasts of Israel detailed in the Torah. It explains why Thyatira, representing Pentecost (Shavuot), marks the beginning of GREAT Tribulation for the wicked.

Do believers today know the appointed times? Not so much.

Paul assumed that his readers know that the "thief in the night" is an allusion to Rosh HaShanah, the Feast of Trumpets, nicknamed *The Day* and *The Hour* that No Man Knows." The decrees of life or death are made on The Day of Rosh HaShanah, and ten days later at Yom HaKippurim, those decrees are sealed for angels to execute. There is a curiosity in Yom HaKippurim, the Day of Atonement. In Hebrew, Yom HaKippurim reads, "a day like Purim."

Purim is the celebration of Queen Esther and Mordechai's heroic victory over Wicked Haman in the Book of Esther. It is called Purim because of the *pur*, or lots, that Haman cast in deciding a day of the Jews' destruction. Likewise, on Yom HaKippurim, the high priest cast lots to decide which goat would have its blood sprinkled in the Holy of Holies and which goat would be sent to Azazel. Ironically, Yom HaKippurim was set in the Biblical calendar long before Purim, yet it is a day *like* Purim, a historical day of deliverance and salvation that hadn't happened yet. The Torah is full of such prophecies.

On Yom HaKippurim, "a day like Purim," in *Maor va'Shemesh*, Rimzei Purim says:

> "...*even the Adversary attests to the righteousness of Israel; our enemy is confounded and turned into our supporter*. That is the symbolism and power of the Ketoret (incense), of taking the putrid-smelling [incense]

helbonah, and creating something pleasant. This is not a confusion of good and evil [like the tree], but the creation of a different compound- an elevation of evil...evil no longer impacts in a negative way; rather evil is co-opted to become an element of good."[71]

What this says is that on Yom HaKippurim, the wicked will be sealed over to destruction and the righteous to salvation and resurrection from the dead. In spite of his evil influence on every other day on the calendar, on Yom HaKippurim, the enemy is confused, and his attempts and plans of evil against the righteous will actually be turned into good, just like the stench of the Tabernacle incense helbonah is turned into something pleasant on the altar.

When it "goes up," the compounded incense mingles with the other spices and the coals from the altar, representing repentance, and the sins of which Israel has repented become a pleasing aroma, acceptable to the Father. What was a horrible stench of sin in His nostrils transforms into the most pleasant perfume of repentant obedience. The satan, or adversary, of sin that accused becomes the advocate with the repentance of Yom HaKippurim.

Beginning in the Biblical month of Elul, it is a Jewish tradition to begin blowing the shofar each day; it is the month prior to Rosh HaShanah and Yom HaKippurim. This is believed to confuse and confound the Adversary, who knows that the sound of the shofar on Rosh HaShanah is the last call to repentance, and his time is short to influence and plan wickedness. If the serpent knows his time is short, perhaps he understands that he has only until an appointed Yom Kippur...or Purim...to deceive the world before his evil is transformed into good for all the righteous and those who repent of unrighteousness.

71. Quoted in Kahn, 2012, p. 261

In light of these traditions, consider John's revelation of the serpent whose time is short:

> And there was war in heaven,
> Michael and his angels waging war
> with the dragon. The dragon and his
> angels waged war, and they were
> not strong enough, and there was
> no longer a place found for them
> in heaven. And the great dragon
> was thrown down, the serpent of old
> who is called the devil and Satan,
> who deceives the whole world; he
> was thrown down to the earth, and
> his angels were thrown down with
> him. Then I heard a loud voice in
> heaven, saying, 'Now the salvation,
> and the power, and the kingdom
> of our God and the authority of His
> Christ [anointed one] have come,
> *for the accuser of our brethren has*
> *been thrown down, he who accuses*
> *them before our God day and night.*
> *And they overcame him because of*
> *the blood of the Lamb and because*
> *of the word of their testimony,* and
> they did not love their life even when
> faced with death. For this reason,
> rejoice, O heavens and you who
> dwell in them. *Woe to the earth*
> *and the sea, because the devil has*
> *come down to you, having great*
> *wrath, knowing that he has only a*
> *short time.*[72]

Rosh HaShanah is celebrated for two days because of the "hiddenness" of THE DAY at the new moon, for the day is determined Biblically by the appearance of the new moon of the Seventh Month. Additionally, Yom HaKippurim is the Day of Judgment. What Rosh HaShanah decrees, Yom Kippur SEALS.

72. Re 12:7-12

> While they are saying, "Peace and safety!" then destruction will come upon them suddenly *like labor pains upon a woman with child*, and they will not escape.

The labor pains are mentioned in Revelation, for both women go to the wilderness for testing. One woman's children will bear the mark of her partner, the beast.[73] The other woman's children have the testimony of Yeshua and the commandments of God.[74] Each year on Rosh HaShanah, Israel is reborn in the synagogue during the prayers/shofar blasts, thus the allusion to labor pains. The people are reborn in a moment when the shofar sounds, in a day.

"The Day" will not overtake the righteous like a thief, for they know the appointed times, especially Rosh HaShanah. They are children of the day, which means that the Light of the Torah and the Lamp of the commandments is shining in them.[75] If the testimony of the Word of God shines from within, then one cannot be in darkness. In fact, one's light is better seen in darkness! This is where the Torah portion *Behaalotkha* is so important ("In your going up"), for it focuses on tending the Menorah, the Lamp of the Spirit. It explains the elevation *Ki Tisa* of the saints at the Feast of Trumpets when the shofar blows at the *Pekudei* reckoning written in the books.

On Day Four of Creation, the sun, moon, and stars, the luminaries, were set in place to govern both the day and night as well as the seasons (*moedim*: appointed times). The appointed times were set as prophecies even before a man was created to learn from them. Later, they were given to Israel as set feast times. For those who desire to be reckoned among the righteous in their going up at the resurrection at the prophesied appointed time, Isaiah writes a reminder of Israel's history of being gathered by the Angel of the Presence of Adonai:

73. Re 17:3

74. Re 12:6, 14

75. Pr 6:23

58

For He said, 'Surely, they are My
people, *sons who will not deal
falsely*.' So He became their Savior.
In all their affliction He was afflicted,
and *the angel of His presence saved
them*; in His love and in His mercy,
He redeemed them, and *He lifted
them and carried them* all the days
of old.[76]

To those children who will not deal falsely, who will
repent with sincerity and behave consistently with
their testimony of Yeshua and the commandments
of God, that invitation into the Presence of the
cloud gathering still stands. Yeshua is the faithful
and true witness, the Son who did not deal falsely
with the Father, but instead, faithfully executed His
commandments.

The Torah's Seed Prophecies

On Day Five of Creation, Elohim created feather-
covered birds and scale-covered fish. They were
called "swarms," indicating a root word (*ratz*) that
connotes huge numbers of rapidly moving feet.

The birds flew above the earth, but within the
breathable air. The fish were *hidden*.

There are two hints: great numbers moving above
the earth, covered, and those that were hidden
from sight to be "fished", but not far away. Likewise,
the righteous dead and living in Yeshua will be
gathered in great numbers into the clouds above on
a hidden day and concealed in a time of tribulation.
The pattern is further established in the exodus from
Egypt:

For the LORD'S portion is His
people; Jacob is the allotment of
His inheritance. He found him in
a desert land, and in the howling

76. Is 63:8-9

59

waste of a wilderness; He encircled
him, He cared for him, He guarded
him as the pupil of His eye. *Like
an eagle* that stirs up its nest, that
hovers over its young, He spread His
wings and caught them, He carried
them on His pinions. The LORD
alone guided him, and there was
no foreign god with him. *He made
him ride on the high places of the
earth...*[77]

This riding high is a specific component of the
Feast of Trumpets, or Rosh HaShanah. It is a day
of remembrance. The Israelites must look to a
past deliverance in order to understand future
ones, specifically the resurrection of the dead at
Rosh HaShanah. Each year the Israelites would be
reminded of the future redemption by recalling the
past:

Speak to the sons of Israel, saying,
'In the seventh month on the first of
the month you shall have a rest, a
reminder by blowing of trumpets, a
holy convocation.'[78]

Rosh HaShanah is a feast of remembrance in the
Jewish tradition. As one of the seven feasts, it is
a rehearsal: *mikra*. It is practice for a prophetic
event. Paul would not have expected his readers
to forget the Feast of Trumpets as a rehearsal for the
resurrection!

In Paul's explanation to the Thessalonians, the Lord
Himself descends from Heaven with a shout and
trumpet, but the saints are caught up. Where is
"up"? With a little investigation into the Greek word
for "air," it doesn't seem as though the air to which
the saints are gathered is that high up. In fact, from
the definition, one respires normally:

77. Dt 32:10-13

78. Le 23:24

60

Strong's #109 *aer* from *aemi* (to
breathe unconsciously, i.e. respire;
by analogy, to blow)

Definition: the air, particularly the
lower and denser air as distinguished
from the higher and rarer air.

Additionally, Jewish expectation as recorded in the
Talmud, Hagigah 5a, is that the Spirit of God is no
higher above the waters than a dove would fly,
which is based on the opening verse of Genesis.
Mark 1:10 matches the expectation of "dove
height"[79]: "Immediately coming up out of the water,
He saw the heavens opening, and the Spirit like a
dove descending upon Him..." Luke 9:35 continues,
"And there came *a voice out of the cloud*, saying,
'This is my beloved Son: hear him." The dove and
the cloud give clues as to the "height" of a realm of
Heaven.

The dove was also the *undivided* offering of the
Covenant Between the Pieces:

It came about *when the sun had set*,
that it was very dark, and behold,
there appeared a smoking oven
and a *flaming torch* which passed
between these pieces.[80]

The pieces were animals that were halved,
forming a mirror image of the other side.
This could represent the nearly identical
blessings promised to Abraham and Sarah[81]
in the covenant. The couple was two, yet they
were one. In a greater sense, it could represent the
righteous woman Israel coming into unity with her
Husband, for the little dove was undivided.

The burning torch appeared when the sun set. This
divided offering preceded the construction of the
Tabernacle or Temple, yet it was prophecy of the

79. Dalman &
Lightfoot, 2002,
p. 65

80. Ge 15:17

81. These paired
blessings will be
discussed in the
BEKY Book *Cave
of the Couples:
What is Really
Buried in Hebron.*

82. The location of Zion will be significant in Section 2 as a hidden "side" of the altar and a place of resurrection. Because Isaiah refuses to "keep silent" until Jerusalem comes forth in brightness, the half-hour of silence in Heaven (Re 8:1) indicates a possible achievement of this Heavenly goal. This is matched by the silence commanded by Moses while the Israelites watch the "salvation" of the Lord while He opens the Reed Sea to draw them forth from the water in that burning, shining salvation and resurrection.

83. The Hebrew term for smoking torch is "esh lapid." The Judge of Israel, Deborah, was married to a man named Lappidot, or "torches," plural. The root of Deborah's name, דבר DVR,

undivided whole burnt offering (olah), morning and evening, of the Tabernacle. This daily offering was tamid, or perpetual. Nothing stopped the evening and morning olah offerings. Olah means "going up."

The evening torch continues burning and purifying the ashes of the evening sacrifice, the first resurrection, through the night until the morning olah, or whole burnt offering, of the second resurrection. In this way, the ashes of the previous resurrection offering were still present at the offering of the next, an uninterrupted prophecy of Abraham's descendants "going up." One side of the pieces mirrored the others, something divided, but yet part of one being. The same fire of resurrection passed through them both. The doves, which also are symbols of resurrection, were whole.

What was this Burning Torch of the Covenant between the pieces? Isaiah 62:1 suggests it was "her salvation," or Yeshua[tah]:

> For Zion's[82] sake I will not keep silent,
> and for Jerusalem's sake I will not
> keep quiet, Until her righteousness
> goes forth like brightness, and her
> salvation like a torch[83] that is burning.

The covenant at Sinai also was made in burning smoke, yet Israel broke the covenant:

> Not according to the covenant that
> I made with their fathers in the day
> that I took them by the hand to bring
> them out of the land of Egypt; which
> my covenant they brake, although I
> was a husband unto them, saith the
> LORD.[84]

Jeremiah speaks of a new covenant in which the Word will be written on the hearts of Israel. Her salvation, Yeshua, came to mediate a better

62

covenant and a better resurrection. By sending the Holy Spirit to write the Word on the hearts of his disciples, he began rebuilding unity between "Husband" Adonai and "Wife" Israel. The Word did not change, Israel did. Since Yeshua appears and disappears clad in garments of smoke, fire, and cloud in the Torah prophecies, we may call him the "hidden" Husband.

With all the talk of trees and birds, consider these passages describing the height of the armies of Heaven:

> It shall be, when you hear the
> sound of marching *in the tops of*
> *the balsam trees*, then you shall act
> promptly, for then the LORD will have
> gone out before you to strike the
> army of the Philistines.[85]

> It shall be when you hear the sound
> of *marching in the tops of the*
> *balsam trees*, then you shall go out
> to battle, for God will have gone out
> before you to strike the army of the
> Philistines.[86]

The balsam trees have a specific context, the Garden of the bride:

> I have come into *my garden, my*
> *sister, my bride; I have gathered* my
> *myrrh* along with my *balsam*.[87]

The lower, earthly balsam trees may represent the balsam trees said in tradition to populate the Lower Garden of Eden. In fact, legend has it that one of the rivers of Eden flows with balsam or balsam perfume. Myrrh smells wonderful when mixed with other scents in a perfume, but alone, like helbonah, it smells pretty skunky! What if Yeshua mixes myrrh, which is a death-spice,[88] with balsam? The result

(83, continued) is also the root of the words for "honeybee" and "Word." The Torah's judgments are sweeter than honey (Ps 19:10; 119:103), so Deborah's place as one of the Torah teachers in the Lower Garden of Eden makes sense, for through her prophetic word, the iron chariots of Israel's enemies were defeated. Her husband Lappidot is wordplay on the *esh lapid*, the burning torch of the Word, Yeshua. Deborah waged war with a man named Barak (lightning). A lightning-like attack on the enemy with the Word is a characteristic worthy of a teacher of Eden.

84. Je 31:32 KJV

85. 2 Sa 5:24

86. 1 Ch 14:15

87. Sng 5:1

would be a wonderful perfume of death mixed with a living tree. The symbolism can't be lost here.

As he promises the repentant thief on the cross, Yeshua will gather the righteous dead in the Lower Garden, called Paradise, and he will perfume the righteous dead with green, living balsam. For David, the height of the marching footsteps of Heaven's armies was in the treetops of earthly balsam trees. How high is Heaven's army? How high will the saints ascend? Although it is a spiritual realm hidden to physical eyes, perhaps it is no higher than a treetop or low-lying cloud. Elisha the Prophet saw into that spiritual realm, and Scripture describes it thus:

> And Elisha prayed, and said, LORD, I pray thee, open his eyes, that he may see. And the LORD opened the eyes of the young man; *and he saw: and, behold, the mountain was full of horses and chariots of fire* round about Elisha.[89]

The wording is odd here. "The mountain" is full of an army of fire *surrounding* Elisha. If the fire *fills* the mountain, then how can it *surround* Elisha? This strange statement will be explained in the context of the fiery Rivers of Eden that surround the Garden of Eden.

88. "Nicodemus, who had first come to Him by night, also came, bringing a **mixture** of myrrh and aloes, about a hundred pounds weight." (Jn 19:39) In Section 2, the principle of the evening *olah* offering burning all night until morning will be explained in further detail as a picture of the resurrection.

89. 2 Ki 6:17 KJV

64

5

THE GARDEN, THE CLOUD, AND THE DEAD

If the Israelites were supposed to believe in Moses forever, then we have a very good reason that Yeshua explained his resurrection beginning with Moses. That's where the seed prophecies were written:

> The LORD said to Moses, "Behold, *I will come to you in a thick cloud*, so that the people may hear when I speak with you and may also *believe in you forever*." Then Moses told the words of the people to the LORD...[90]

The people need to believe in Moses forever because in the Song of Moses in Revelation 15:3, they are still singing his song! Also, the "thick cloud" is a prophecy of the Garden of Eden, or Paradise, where according to Jewish tradition and Yeshua's words on the cross, the souls of the righteous dead await the first resurrection: "In *Gan Eden* [Garden of Eden], from the wall inward, there is a thick cloud, but its surroundings are brilliant."[91] This brilliant cloud calls to mind the brilliant cloud that enveloped Yeshua, Moses, and Elijah on the Mount

90. Ex 19:9

91. Raphael, 2009, p. 199

65

of Transfiguration, a vision so clear that the disciples wanted to build Sukkot (Tabernacles).

The Jericho Prophecy

When the Israelites concluded their wilderness wandering, they had to cross the Jordan River. In Hebrew, Jordan is *Yarden*, which means "descent." Yeshua was immersed in the Yarden, telling his cousin John that it served a purpose, signaling that the Father's favor would descend on him in a special way and that Yeshua would descend in a special way at his second coming.

Paul assured the Thessalonians that the Lord would descend with a shout to meet the Beloved and gather her into the Lower Garden, or Paradise, at the resurrection. Israel, then, is a physical land that represents a spiritual reality of resurrection. By seeing the physical land, one sees a picture of the Lower Garden, which is just above it.

A miracle accompanied the Israelites' entrance into the Land of Israel under the leadership of Joshua. It was a miracle similar to the crossing of the Reed Sea in the Exodus from Egypt. Psalm 114 implies that at the same time that Israel left Egypt, the Yarden River ran backward, a fact repeated every year at the family Passover seder:

> When Israel went forth from Egypt,
> the house of Jacob from a people of
> strange language, Judah became
> His sanctuary; Israel, His dominion.
> The sea looked and fled; the Jordan
> turned back. The mountains skipped
> like rams; the hills, like lambs. What
> ails you, O sea, that you flee? O
> Jordan, that you turn back?[92]

92. Ps 114:1-5 A body of water that normally flowed downward through Israel to Jericho, and then on to the

valley of Sodom and Gomorrah, suddenly reversed direction, going up. It came down, then it went up. Strangely, it piled up like a pillar all the way to a city called Adam, about 30 miles upriver from their crossing place at Zarethan[93] near Sukkot[94] and Jericho.

The Israelites crossed this river on an anniversary of their exodus from Egypt. Until the destruction in Abraham's generation, this same river made the plain of Sodom and Gomorrah "eastward"[95] into a well-watered beautiful garden like Eden and like the irrigated gardens of Egypt:

> Lot lifted up his eyes and saw all the valley of the Jordan, that it was well watered everywhere—this was before the LORD destroyed Sodom and Gomorrah—*like the garden* of the LORD, like the land of Egypt as you go to Zoar.[96]

After the geological destruction, the Yarden River emptied in the Salt Sea, or Dead Sea, a deep basin of salt water which heaved up in an earthquake that likely accompanied the fire and brimstone.[97]

> So when the people set out from their tents to cross the Jordan with the priests carrying the ark of the covenant before the people, and when those who carried the ark came into the Jordan, and the feet of the priests carrying the ark were dipped in the edge of the water (for the Jordan overflows all its banks all the days of harvest), *the waters which were flowing down from above stood and rose up in one heap*, a great distance away at Adam, the city that is beside Zarethan; and those which

93. For an explanation of the prophetic significance of Zarethan and Sukkot, see *Creation Gospel Workbook One*, section "Heaven's Gold in a Clay Mold."

94. Solomon later cast the metal vessels for the First Temple in the clay of the plain between Zarethan and Sukkot. Metal vessels do not have to be destroyed if they become ritually impure, but can be passed through water and fire and restored to holy use.

95. The LORD God planted a garden *toward the east*, in Eden; and there He placed the man whom He had formed. Ge 2:8

96. Ge 13:10

97. Bohrer, 2007, pp. 201-202

were flowing down toward the sea of the Arabah, the Salt Sea, were completely cut off. So the people crossed opposite Jericho. And the priests who carried the ark of the covenant of the LORD stood firm on dry ground in the middle of the Jordan while all Israel crossed on dry ground, until all the nation had finished crossing the Jordan.[98]

At Mount Sinai, the Israelites were shown that they were not yet ready to "go up," yet the Presence and the voice descended upon them. When they heard the ram's horn, only then could they go up:

> "...You shall set bounds for the people all around, saying, 'Beware that you do not go up on the mountain or touch the border of it; whoever touches the mountain shall surely be put to death. No hand shall touch him, but he shall surely be stoned or shot through; whether beast or man, he shall not live. *When* the **ram's horn** (*yovel*) sounds a long blast, **they shall come up** to the mountain.'"[99]

Likewise, when Israel crossed the Jordan, it was a prophecy of Yeshua descending to meet them. They approached the first city, Jericho. Like the boundary at Sinai was a red light until the ram's horn sounded, so the boundary of Jericho's walls stood until the green light of the ram's horn blast. At that point, Israel could ascend into the city and the Land of Israel, prophecy of Paradise. The Israelites circled Jericho, simulating the movement of the circular rivers of Eden.

98. Jo 3:14-17

99. Ex 19:13

> Now Jericho was tightly shut because of the sons of Israel; *no*

68

*one went out and no one came
in.* The LORD said to Joshua, 'See, I
have given Jericho into your hand,
with its king and the valiant warriors.
You shall march around the city,
all the men of war circling the city
once. You shall do so for six days.
Also *seven priests shall carry seven
trumpets of rams' horns (yovlim)
before the ark; then on the seventh
day you shall march around the city
seven times, and the priests shall
blow the trumpets (shofar)...*

The shofars are heralds, trumpets at the appointed times, the seven feasts of Israel. When the prophetic cycle of the seven feasts is finally completed, Jericho will be "in your hand." Each feast prophesies of some aspect of the Divine plan of salvation, deliverance, resurrection, and restoration of human beings to the domain of the first Adam in the Garden of Eden, Paradise. The voice of Adonai emanated from between the two cherubim of the Ark in the Holy of Holies of the Tabernacle. To break through to Jericho, the voice traveled in circles around it, simulating those circling rivers of Eden, which represent the Spirit of Adonai.[100] They are the rivers to which Yeshua referred when he stood at the Feast of Tabernacles and said,

> Now on the last day, the great day
> of the feast, Jesus stood and cried
> out, saying, 'If anyone is thirsty, let
> him come to Me and drink.'[101]

Yeshua proclaimed himself to be the "breakthrough" that mankind needed to return to the Garden, to be resurrected from the barriers of death, hell, and the grave. Through the "voice" of Yeshua speaking the Word of the Father as at Sinai, the walls would fall so that passage would open for Israel and they could ascend to the Garden.

100. See *Creation Gospel Workbook Five: Volume One, Bereishit,* for a complete explanation of the Rivers of Eden as the encircling of God's Spirit.

101. Jn 7:37

...It shall be that when they make **a long blast with the ram's (*yovel*) horn (*keren*)**, and when you hear the sound of the trumpet (*shofar*), all the people shall **shout with a great shout**; and the wall of the city will fall down flat, and **the people will go up every man** straight ahead." (Joshua 6:1-6)

Keren can mean a ray of light, power, or a literal horn. Resurrection is often referred to as "resurrection power," for such a transformation of the human body requires the power of the Holy Spirit. This fifth feast, Rosh HaShanah, corresponds to the fifth Spirit of Adonai listed in Isaiah 11:2, which is Power. Even the Jewish name for the Feast of Trumpets, Rosh HaShanah, hints to what happens on that day. Although it literally means "the head of the year," the root of *shanah* means "change." The graphic below demonstrates *when* and *how* resurrection into the clouds of glory occurs:

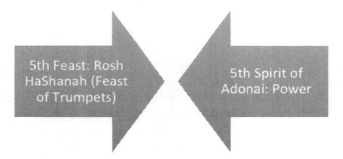

5th Feast: Rosh HaShanah (Feast of Trumpets)

5th Spirit of Adonai: Power

The shouting blast of the ram's horn on the Feast of Trumpets was a long, powerful blast. It is referred to as the day of the awakening blast, or literally, *Yom Teruah*, the Day of Blowing.[102] The resurrection trumpets call to the righteous at Rosh HaShanah to undergo their change into an immortal body, and the Yovlim (plural of shofar) seal them in their new-life bodies on Yom HaKippurim ten days later. This explains why Israel needed to believe in Moses forever. The Revelation of John is

102. The Feast of Trumpets is also known as Yom Teruah, Rosh HaShana, The Day of Blowing, or the Day of the Awakening Blast

70

the Revelation at Sinai fulfilled, and so many other TANAKH[103] prophecies as well.

For instance, the Jericho *yovel* is associated with the time of Passover:

> Now when they had finished
> circumcising all the nation, they
> remained in their places in the camp
> until they were healed. Then the
> LORD said to Joshua, 'Today I have
> rolled_away the reproach of Egypt
> from you.' So the name of that place
> is called Gilgal to this day. While
> the sons of Israel camped at *Gilgal,*
> *they observed the Passover on*
> *the evening of the fourteenth day*
> *of the month on the desert plains*
> *of Jericho.* On the day after the
> Passover, on that very day, they ate
> some of the produce of the land,
> unleavened cakes and parched
> grain.[104]

Gilgal means "rolling or circling." In Modern Hebrew, a tire is a *galgal*. Like the rivers of Eden, the naming of Gilgal reflects the circular path of the appointed times. The Israelites will cross into this special physical Promised Land after the feast of Passover. The physical Land of Israel is a step toward entering into the spiritual home of the Lower Garden above it. At Jericho, this crossing over was marked by the blast of the *yovel*, or ram's horn. Yovel is also the Hebrew word for the English "Jubilee," a year of release and return to one's original home, picturing a return to the Garden of Eden.

The Jubilee is based on counting time periods of sevens, and it is given a footprint in both spring and fall feast seasons. Even the weekly Shabbat is a Little Jubilee in which to share with others.

103. Old Testament

104. Jo 5: 9-11

> (Spring **Week** of) Passover: Jericho 7, 7, 7x7
>
> ▸Shavuot[105]: Feast of **Weeks** 7x7
>
> (Autumn **Week** of) Sukkot: Shmittah[106] and Jubilee 7, 7x7

Shavuot happens annually. After the Passover celebration of Firstfruits, seven weeks are counted to a yearly jubilee, Shavuot, or Feast of Weeks. The Feast of Weeks joins two other feasts of weeks, Passover in the Spring and Sukkot in the Autumn[107]. To learn about "the Day of the Lord," a believer needs to jump into the cycle of the Biblical feasts each year. The beauty of a circle is that there is no starting or stopping place. A person can jump in on any day on the calendar, move with the power of the Holy Spirit, and become part of the reckoning at the time of going up. Yeshua extended this invitation to all, for Shavuot has a special invitation for the Gentile to join the Jew at the celebration.[108]

The Firstfruits of Wheat is celebrated at Shavuot. It is a celebration of produce, for Adonai says, "the Land is MINE." This is an open door even to those WITHOUT an inheritance in the Land: stranger, alien, orphan, widow, and Levite.[109] The Book of Ruth is read in synagogues on the day of Shavuot. Its story covers the time between the Firstfruits of the Barley at Passover and the Firstfruits of the Wheat at Shavuot. It was then that the righteous non-Jew Ruth was invited to join the circle with the Jews Naomi and Boaz in the Land of Israel. Ruth says,

> Do not urge me to leave you or turn back from following you; for where you go, I will go, and where you lodge, I will lodge. Your people shall be my people, and your God, my God. *Where you die, I will die, and there I will be buried.* Thus may

105. Pentecost

106. Year of release for Hebrew indentured servants.

107. See Figure 1

108. For an overview of the Biblical calendar, see S. Creeger's *Growing in Holiness: The Hebrew Calendar Day by Day.*

109. The Levites were not given an inheritance of tillable or grazing land, but of refuge cities.

the LORD do to me, and worse, if
anything but death parts you and
me."[110]

Naomi and Boaz were from Bethlehem. A savior
would arise from there, a savior that would gather
many from the nations into the circling Rivers of Eden.
As Yeshua told the Samaritan woman, "Salvation is
from the Jews."[111] Ruth recognizes her prophetic role,
and her persistence in matters of salvation and hope
in the resurrection of the dead draw her into the
Garden circle of the feasts, forever memorialized in
the celebration of Shavuot. She was an ancestress
of King David and the Messiah.

Passover week includes Firstfruits of the Barley. Before
Yeshua's death, burial, and resurrection during the
Passover week, the transfiguration occurs with Moses
and Elijah, an event that spurs the three disciples to
offer building Sukkot (booths, tabernacles) on the site.
Passover and Sukkot are joined by Shavuot, the little
jubilee. Luke 9:30-31 describes the transfiguration:

> And behold, there talked with him
> two men, which were Moses and
> Elijah; who appeared in glory, and
> spoke of his decease which he was
> about to accomplish at Jerusalem.

The word "decease" in Greek is "exodus," linking
Yeshua's impending death, burial, and resurrection
to the Exodus from Egypt.[112] Sukkot week includes
tithes of diverse kinds of produce and livestock, and
it reiterates the message of sharing with stranger,
alien, orphan, widow, and Levite, those who have
no inheritance in the Land.

Are there other examples of the cloud coming
down?

> And it came about when the priests
> came from the holy place, that the

110. Ru 1:16-17

111. Jn 4:22

112. Dalman, p.
106

cloud filled the house of the LORD,
so that the priests could not stand
to minister *because of the cloud*, for
the glory of the LORD filled the house
of the LORD. Then Solomon said,
*'The LORD has said that He would
dwell in the thick cloud.'*[113]

Paul writes something that he did not expect would be a surprise, something that he says is by the Word of the Lord. In other words, disciples of Yeshua should already have context for the event designed for them to "ever be with the Lord." It was the building of the Tabernacle that was a teaching focal point and for the Holy One to dwell among Israel in a thick cloud:

"And let them make me a sanctuary;
that I may dwell among them."[114]

And there **I will meet** with the
children of Israel, and the tabernacle
shall be sanctified by **my glory**. And
I will sanctify the tabernacle of the
congregation, and the altar: I will
sanctify also both Aaron and his
sons, **to minister to me in the priest's
office**. And **I will dwell among the
children of Israel**, and will be their
God. And they shall know that I am
the LORD their God, that brought
them forth **out of the land of Egypt,
that I may dwell among them**: I am
the LORD their God.
115

The Tabernacle was a place of dwelling with the glory of Adonai, forever memorialized by its precipitating event, the exodus from Egypt. Within context, the priesthood of Aaron is mentioned.

The LORD said to Moses, *'Behold, I
will come to you in a thick cloud, so*

113. 1 Ki 8:10-12

114. Ex 25:8

115. Ex 29:43-46

*that the people may hear when I
speak with you and may also believe
in you forever.' Then Moses told the
words of the people to the LORD.*[116]

On Yom Kippur, the high priest takes the clouds of incense into the Holy of Holies. It is a day on which the Divine Cloud joins with the clouds of the prayers of the People of Israel. It is a day of intimacy in the cloud signified by the mirrored (chiastic) cherubim over the ark. In the Jewish tradition, they represented a male and female. Whether they literally had that form is not known, but the spiritual picture of intimacy is the point of the tradition. The *Cohen HaGadol* (High Priest) brings the cloud of incense, representing the repentant prayers of Israel, and it merges with the Divine Presence that hovered over the ark in the Cloud. The two clouds become one.

Shabbat is understood in Judaism to be a type of wedding ring identifying the Bride Israel. The physical intimacy of marriage is a Shabbat tradition, a parable of the spiritual intimacy with the King by the Bride.[117]

One wears fine clothes on Shabbat just as on the High Sabbaths of the Biblical feasts, for it is the expectation of a wedding invitation. As one dresses on Shabbat, it reflects an expectation that the prophecy of The Day will be fulfilled. One desires to enter the cloud on Rosh HaShanah, be sealed in marriage at Yom HaKippurim, and enjoy the wedding feast at Sukkot.

Jesus spoke to them again in parables, saying, 'The kingdom of heaven may be compared to a king who gave a wedding feast for his son. And he sent out his slaves to call those who had been invited to the wedding feast, and they were unwilling to come. Again he sent out other slaves saying, 'Tell those

116. Ex 19:7-9

117. There is also a Queen of Shabbat tradition that presents another aspect.

who have been invited, "Behold, I
have prepared my dinner; my oxen
and my fattened livestock are *all
butchered and everything is ready;
come to the wedding feast."* But
they paid no attention and went
their way, one to his own farm,
another to his business, and the rest
seized his slaves and mistreated
them and killed them. But the king
was enraged, and he sent his armies
and destroyed those murderers and
set their city on fire.

Then he said to his slaves, 'The
wedding is ready, but those who
were invited were not worthy. *Go
therefore to the main highways,
and as many as you find there,
invite to the wedding feast.'* Those
slaves went out into the streets
and gathered together all they
found, both evil and good; and the
wedding hall was filled with dinner
guests. *But when the king came in to
look over the dinner guests, he saw
a man there who was not dressed in
wedding clothes,* and he said to him,
'Friend, how did you come in here
without wedding clothes?' And the
man was speechless.

Then the king said to the servants,
'Bind him hand and foot, and throw
him into the outer darkness; in that
place there will be weeping and
gnashing of teeth.' For many are
called, but few *are chosen.*"[118]

The Shabbat is the weekly wedding in Jewish tradition;
it prepares the chosen...and those who choose to
attend...for the great wedding feast at Sukkot, the

118. Mt 22:1-14

Seventh Day. Although both evil and good guests are invited, it is not an excuse to choose to refuse the sanctification of commandments or continued works of repentance. Yeshua's work is not looking the other way when those who attend his feasts do so without coming in clothes of commandments with repentance. Yeshua died for those wedding clothes.

White garments are prominent both in tradition and Scripture. They symbolize obedience to the Heavenly Throne. A message to the assembly of Laodicea in Revelation hints to this need for obedience.

> And I saw the dead, the great and the small, standing before the throne, and books were opened; and another *book was opened, which is the book of life*; and the dead were judged from the things which were written in the books, *according to their deeds.* And the sea gave up the dead which were in it, and death and Hades gave up the dead which were in them; and they were judged, every one *of them* according to their deeds.[119]

Each person has a book in which his or her deeds are written. Those deeds are measured against what is written in the Book of Life, and a judgment is rendered. The dead come from both the earth (Hades) and the sea.

119. Re 20:12–13

6

FIREMEN AND ROBES OF RIGHTEOUSNESS

The message to the last assembly of Revelation, Laodicea, is written in memo format, not a letter. A memo is designed for people inside the work environment. In modern terms, an interoffice memo is sent to people who already work for the company; they know what is to be produced; they know who the boss and supervisors are; they know the work and break times; they know the problems within the company; and they know what is considered a success, both in one's own particular job and in relation to the whole company. A memo is for people who are already familiar with its context, but they need reminders or additional instructions.

To: Laodicea Tabernacles – Adat Shabbat/Sukkot

From: The Amen, the faithful and true Witness, the Beginning of the creation of God

Creative Clean Works of the Spirit of Reverence: None mentioned

(continued on next page...)

Unclean Works: I know your deeds, that you are neither cold nor hot; I would that you were cold or hot. So because you are lukewarm, and neither hot nor cold, I will spit you out of My mouth.

Commands: Because you say, "I am rich, and have become wealthy, and have need of nothing," and you do not know that you are wretched and miserable and poor and blind and naked, I advise you to buy from Me gold refined by fire, that you may become rich, and white garments, that you may clothe yourself, and that the shame of your nakedness may not be revealed; and eye salve to anoint your eyes, that you may see. Those whom I love, I reprove and discipline; be zealous therefore, and repent.

Exhortation: Behold, I stand at the door and knock; if anyone hears My voice and opens the door, I will come in to him, and will dine with him, and he with Me. He who overcomes, I will grant to him to sit down with Me on My throne, as I also overcame and sat down with My Father on His throne. He who has an ear, let him hear what the Spirit says to the churches.

Keeping commandments is for growth in salvation, not salvation itself, and obedience to the commandments is Yeshua's righteousness, not the individual's. It is Messiah's righteous clothes of living obedience that one acquires and wears to clothe nakedness. Believers live *in* Yeshua's clothes of the commandments, but they are not the manufacturers of them. The righteous acquire them with faithfulness to live as he did. Moses instructed the Israelites, "And you shall *live* by them…" *Veh-chai b'hem*. The implication is that once saved, just as the Israelites were saved from Egypt, then the commandments create a climate favorable for growth in new life after deliverance.

It is important not to confuse salvation in Yeshua with deeds of faithfulness to the Savior. In Yeshua, the believer is born again through no effort of his or her own, just as a baby is born into this world through no effort of his own. As the mother endures birth pangs, so Messiah's suffering and tribulation brought forth salvation for all who would embrace that rebirth.

Being born, however, is not an accomplishment that most adults proclaim frequently. Instead, infants grow to maturity, and while they may rejoice at the opportunity to live and enjoy life, they recognize that living requires growth in deeds, not simply basking in the gift of existence. Similarly, believers should be eternally grateful for the gift of salvation, but life requires living and growing. This is the function of the commandments, for one is to live IN them, not to be born of them. Failing to walk in one's faith is equivalent to an infant never taking his first steps! Salvation is not based on works, but growing to adulthood is dependent upon good and diligent work.

In Yeshua's parable of the man in filthy clothes at the wedding feast, one's garment at the King's table is important. The Laodiceans were likewise warned that they needed white garments so that their nakedness would not be revealed. When Adam and Eve sinned, it was *then* that they knew they were naked. A commandment obeyed is "clothes," but a commandment disobeyed removes that garment. In the rabbinic tradition, Adam and Eve were clothed in light, but when they sinned, the glory departed, and they received animal skins. COVERED THEIR SIN

From the Messianic perspective, perhaps they were clothed in the skin of the Lamb who was slain from the foundation of the world[120] to cover their shame. That same Lamb is very committed to restoring garments of white light to his disciples, for the Torah is a light, and the commandment is a lamp. Human beings were created to be more than clay lamps "under

120. Re 13:8

a basket"; they were created to be living, lifted-up lamps for the Light.

In the Garden of Eden, there was black onyx stone,[121] a precious stone found in the place of "Good Gold." Onyx in Hebrew is *shoham*, but its root means "to turn white." These black...no white...stones[122] were found inside the circling Rivers of Eden. A river in Hebrew means "burning and shining." The Rivers of Eden were burning fire fed by the River that flowed out of Heavenly Eden. Grammatically, the Good Gold in Genesis Two is a proper name/noun, not an adjective modifying a common noun as usually translated. Good Gold prophesies of a people who will inhabit the Garden. Now re-read:

Revelation 3:18 urges:

> I advise you *to buy from Me* gold refined by fire so that you may become rich, and *white garments so that you may clothe yourself, and that the shame of your nakedness will not be revealed...*"

Although John writes in Greek, the Hebrew cognate verb for "to buy" is *liknot*, and it has a dual meaning of "to acquire," not only to pay money. Good works cannot be bought, but there is a price to acquire them, which is the suffering of obedience.[123]

In Jewish tradition, the commandments become spiritual clothes for the afterlife, and without them, one experiences shame at judgment when the books are opened, for there are no matching deeds of "life" from the Book of Life in their books. Transgressions are stains that must be "bleached" from those clothes through confession and repentance.

Adonai assures His people that though their sins are like scarlet that He will make them as white as snow;[124] Adonai will accept their repentance and

121. Ge 2:12

122. Yeshua promises his faithful that they will receive this white stone in Revelation 2:17.

123. Although He was a Son, He learned obedience from the things which He suffered. (Heb. 5:8)

82

forgive their transgressions. Jewish Law considers snow a primary cleansing agent (hamlaben) along with water.[125] Observance of the commandments and repentance help a disciple of Yeshua to stay clothed in Yeshua and raise awareness of transgressions, so by all means, remain clothed! Obedience honors the blood shed by Messiah and prevents the shame of nakedness at the judgment. The outer spiritual river of Eden, the Pishon River, is thought to be represented by the physical Nile River, where flax grew along its banks for linen, which is shesh in Hebrew.

The linen garments worn by the priests of the Temple were made of shesh:

Strong's #8336 שש shesh

Definition: **something bleached white**, byssus, fine linen, alabaster

---

Linen, or shesh, is written by a doubled Hebrew letter shin. The letter shin represents the shen, teeth, and shon, the tongue. In Scripture, the shon (tongue) is a "fire."[126] The doubled shin illustrates the whiteness of the linen as well as its fire and the number six, the number of man and beast, who were created on the Sixth Day of Creation. The priests ministered in linen garments of figurative fire-fire! As the fiery rivers surrounded Eden, so the priests reminded Israel of their restoration to Good Gold and their need for white garments. Twice does Israel see this reminder of fiery tongues as a symbol of restoration to the Garden.

The first was at Mount Sinai, when Israel "saw" the sounds of the fire on the mountain. They received the commandments of Adonai at that time, responding, "We will do, and we will hear." According to rabbinic tradition, the 70 symbolic nations of the world all received the offer of the covenant at the sound of

124. Is 1:18

125. Appel, p. 153

126. Is 30:27; Ja 3:5-6

the shofar, but only Israel accepted as a nation.[127] The second time was in Acts Two, where once again fire fell from Heaven in the form of cloven tongues. Those celebrating the Feast of Shavuot in the Temple began to speak in the languages of the world in those tongues. The shofar of the ram caught in the thicket is an ubiquitous symbol of Shavuot, and the *Akeidah*, or binding of Isaac is read as a reminder of resurrection. What does a cloven tongue of fire look like? A Hebrew letter *shin*! Fire-fire!

127. The Jewish sages also say that Moses expounded the Torah to the Israelites in the 70 languages of the world (Lichtman, 2006, p. 319).

7

YESHUA IN THE EXODUS CLOUD

It is in the Book of Exodus that so much information is detailed about the resurrection of the dead. In a previous chapter, the linguistic connection was established between Yeshua's resurrection and the Greek word "exodus." The title of the Book of Exodus was not originally Exodus, though. In Hebrew, it is Shemot, which means "names." The names are the children of Israel who left Egypt. They were the increase from the tribes, and they were accounted or reckoned from the original 70 Israelites who went from the Promised Land down to Egypt:

> These are the *names* of the sons of Israel who came to Egypt with Jacob, each with his household: Reuben, Simeon, Levi, and Judah, Issachar, Zebulun, and Benjamin, Dan and Naphtali, Gad and Asher. *All the descendants of Jacob were seventy persons*; Joseph was already in Egypt. Then Joseph died, and all his brothers and all that generation. But the people of Israel were fruitful and increased greatly; they multiplied and grew exceedingly strong, so that the land was filled with them.[128]

128. Ex 1:1-7

When the Israelite "names" made their exodus from Egypt, their numbers had greatly increased, and a mixed multitude from other nations also left with them, all covered with a garment of salvation. Once they entered the wilderness, they were given the commandments to increase in holiness so that they could enter the Promised Land, a physical land representing the Garden. The resurrection hints increase in Shemot, the Book of Exodus. In this book of the Torah, the activity of the cloud clarifies the process of resurrection.

The Exodus Torah Portion *Pekudei* means "accounting" or "reckoning." If an Israelite or one of the mixed multitude wanted to be reckoned in the cloud, then the following verses from Pekudei give a glimpse into it:

> Then *the cloud covered* the tent of
> meeting, and *the glory of the LORD
> filled the tabernacle*. Moses was not
> able to enter the tent of meeting
> because *the cloud had settled
> on it*, and *the glory of the LORD
> filled the tabernacle*. Throughout
> all their journeys whenever *the
> cloud* was taken up from over the
> tabernacle, the sons of Israel would
> set out; but if *the cloud* was not
> taken up, then they did not set out
> until the day when it was taken up.
> For throughout all their journeys,
> *the cloud* of the LORD was on the
> tabernacle by day, and there was
> *fire in it by night, in the sight of all the
> house of Israel*. (Ex 40:34-38)

"The cloud" is the repetitious phrase, appearing four times in a few verses, a very small neighborhood for that many sightings. The cloud is characterized by an indwelling Presence of the LORD, filling, and glory. There was fire in the cloud by night, and everyone could see it! The cloud was not out of sight. The movement of the cloud determined where Israel camped and when they moved. It is very similar to the four living creatures that moved wherever the Spirit wanted to go in Ezekiel:

> When the living creatures went, the wheels went beside them; and when the living creatures were lifted up from the earth, the wheels were *lifted up. Wherever the spirit wanted to go, they went, because there the spirit went;* and the wheels were lifted together with them, for the spirit of the living creatures was in the wheels. When those went, these went; when those stood, these stood; and when those were *lifted up from the earth,* the wheels were lifted up together with them, for the spirit of the living creatures was in the wheels.[129]

Wheels within the wheel describes the *saviv* movement of the spiritual Rivers of Eden. Those who dwelled within the river-wheels of Eden could "lift up" if that was the will of the Spirit. The four living creatures of ox, lion, man, and eagle were the four standards by which the twelve tribes of Israel camped and moved. Within the "wheels" of Eden, there was life and spirit. It is believed that before sin, Adam and Eve had the ability to pass between the physical and spiritual, or heavenly, realms of the Garden of Eden. In their special garments of light, they could lift up within the wheels of the Garden rivers.

Psalm 104:1-4 describes the light garments and cloud-walking ability that the first couple may have enjoyed before their sin:

Bless the LORD, O my soul! O LORD

129. Ezek 1:19-21

my God, You are very great; You are
clothed with splendor and majesty,
*covering Yourself with light as with
a cloak*, stretching out heaven like
a tent curtain. He lays the beams of
His *upper chambers in the waters*;
He makes the *clouds His chariot*; He
walks upon the wings of the wind;
He makes the winds His messengers,
flaming fire His ministers.

Heaven is *shamayim* in Hebrew, a blend of the letter *shin*, which represents fire, and *mayim*, which is water. The wilderness cloud that guided the Israelites was composed of both water and fire. A pillar, *amud*, has the implication of something firmly established and standing, *amad*, in Hebrew. This heavenly establishment nevertheless moved at a level that could be seen by each Israelite on the journey, whether by day or night.

In that fire-water cloud, there were special "clothes" required of splendor and light. In those cloud waters were the "beams" of the Holy One's "upper chambers." Likewise, Moses glowed with a splendid light, suggesting that he'd tapped into the lower chambers of the cloud waters where the foundational beams stood. The same word for the cloak-light אוֹר in the Psalm describes the rays of light shining from Moses' face after he spoke with Adonai.

Moses needed a special light garment to endure even in the Presence of the lower chambers. Likewise, the priests had to wear special garments in the Tabernacle for "splendor and glory." They mediated for Israel between heaven and earth, teaching them the instructions of the Torah so that their days would be long. The upper chambers described in Psalm 104 is עֲלִיּוֹתָיו (*aliyotav*). A simple translation is "His going-up place, ascent."

You shall make holy garments for

> Aaron your brother, for glory (kvod)
> and for beauty (tiferet).[130]
>
> For Aaron's sons you shall make
> tunics; you shall also *make sashes* for
> them, and you shall make caps for
> them, for glory (kvod) and for beauty
> (tiferet).[131]

The garments represented a temporary way for man to cling to their Creator in His upper chambers even though they were still confined to the physical earth. The splendid garments of white were necessary, for the priests ministered in the glory of the Tabernacle and the Temple. Some of that glory of the lower chamber clouds and fire was imparted to them to encourage Israel, who would in turn encourage the nations to turn back to their Creator and forsake other gods who could never return them to the glory and beauty of the Lower Garden called Eden.

> 'For *as the waistband clings to the*
> *waist of a man*, so I made the whole
> household of Israel and the whole
> household of Judah cling to Me,'
> declares the LORD, 'that they might
> be for Me a people, for renown, for
> praise and for glory (tiferet); but they
> did not listen.'[132]

There is an aspect of the cloud that is not so much fun to think about, but necessary. Those who dwell there must be able to meet a stricter standard of judgment, thus the concern for holiness. If Adam and Eve fell out of the Garden because of sin, a return to the Garden in sin wouldn't be wise. For forty years in the wilderness, the Israelites were educated in holiness, acquiring Yeshua's garments, the holy commandment. They learned to obey the Father, which meant they had to obey the judgment of the Angel in the cloud, who had the Divine Name and voice within him.

130. Ex 28:2

131. Ex 28:40

132. Je 13:11

> Behold, I am going to send an angel
> before you to guard you along the
> way and to bring you into the place
> which I have prepared. Be on your
> guard before him and *obey his
> voice; do not be rebellious toward
> him, for he will not pardon your
> transgression, since My Name is in
> him.* But if you truly *obey his voice*
> and do all that I say, then I will be
> an enemy to your enemies and an
> adversary to your adversaries.[133]

That Angel protected them on the journey and brought them to the Land of Israel, a place of resurrection, but the prerequisite was obedience. They may have been a people saved from Egypt, but it did not transform them immediately into a holy, obedient nation fit for a resurrection Garden. The transgressions still residing within them would make their residence in the Promised Land short. It was only Moses who achieved a glow of light radiating from his face in his intimacy with the voice and commandments.

The Angel in the Cloud had a special attribute and ability, the power to forgive sin. This was a power of judgment assigned to him by the Holy One. This power of forgiving or not forgiving sin was important, for the Angel was tasked with guiding and protecting Israel until they reached the Holy Land.

> The LORD said to Moses, '*Whoever
> has sinned against Me, I will blot
> him out of My book.* But go now,
> lead the people where I told you.
> Behold, *My angel shall go before
> you;* nevertheless *in the day when I
> punish,* I will punish them for their sin.'
> Then the LORD smote the people,
> because of what they did with the
> calf which Aaron had made.[134]

133. Ex 23:20-22

134. Ex 32:33-35

The Angel was sent with judgment power. There were books in Heaven that recorded the deeds of each individual. The books were still open until "The Day" of punishment for sin. Strangely, "the LORD smote the people" because of the Golden Calf, so it seems as if there were two punishments, one immediate, and one to be administered in "the day." Among all the possible explanations, perhaps the Holy One is pointing out that there are immediate consequences for sin, yet there remains a judgment at the resurrection. The judgment of "The Day" would be the more serious, for it could result in one's name being blotted out of the Book of Life.

The Angel of the Divine Presence played a role in leading Israel. He would not pardon for rebellious, and we might assume, un-repented sins. He could not, for he had to act according to the will of the Divine Name and power within him. If he had the power *not* to pardon rebellious sin, then the obverse should be true: he had the power to forgive a repentant sinner.

This delegated power to forgive, or not forgive, transgressions appears again in Messiah Yeshua:

> I have come as *Light* into the world,
> so that everyone who believes in Me
> will not remain in darkness. *If anyone*
> *hears My sayings and does not keep*
> *them, I do not judge him;* for I did
> not come to judge the world, but to
> save the world. *He who rejects Me*
> *and does not receive My sayings,*
> *has one who judges him; the word*
> *I spoke is what will judge him at*
> *the last day. For I did not speak on*
> *My own initiative, but the Father*
> *Himself who sent Me has given Me*
> *a commandment as to what to say*
> *and what to speak. I know that*
> *His commandment is eternal life;*

therefore, the things I speak, *I speak just as the Father has told Me*.[135]

Yeshua identifies himself with the Torah, the Father's instructions to His children Israel, for the "Torah is a Light, and the commandment is a Lamp." The Angel of the Presence had the authority of the Father in the wilderness to speak His Word, and the Angel's Presence was binding because the Name, and therefore the deeds, of the Father were in him. The Angel did not speak of his own initiative, but reflected exactly the living Word of the Father by which Israel was judged. Yeshua identifies himself according to this "cloud" pattern and reminds his listeners that the same Word will judge them in the last day.

> And they brought to Him a paralytic lying on a bed. Seeing their faith, Jesus said to the paralytic, 'Take courage, son; *your sins are forgiven*.' And some of the scribes said to themselves, '*This fellow blasphemes*.' And Jesus knowing their thoughts said, 'Why are you thinking evil in your hearts? Which is easier, to say, "'Your sins are forgiven,'" or to say, "'Get up, and walk'"?
>
> ...*But so that you may know that the Son of Man has authority on earth to forgive sins*'-then He said to the paralytic, 'Get up, pick up your bed and go home.' And he got up and went home. But when the crowds saw this, they were awestruck, and *glorified God, who had given such authority to men.*[136]

The crowd's reaction is significant. Yeshua was a man, yet he had authority to forgive, so he was no ordinary human being. They were awestruck by this authority, which had been given to the Angel of the

135. Jn 12:46–50

136. Mt 9:2-8

Holy One's Presence to lead Israel home. The royal throne authority of the Divine Name within the Angel of the Presence, Yeshua, is written of in the Psalms, and the traditional language of the fall feasts is found in those verses.

Progressive Mention in Psalm 47 links the traditional Jewish theme of Rosh HaShanah, the authority of the throne and kingship, to the sound of the shofar:

> God has ascended with a shout, the LORD, with the sound of a trumpet (shofar). (5)
>
> God reigns over the nations, God sits on His holy throne. (8)
>
> For the LORD Most High is to be feared, a great King over all the earth. (2)

The prayers of the synagogue during Rosh HaShanah repetitively mention the themes of the King's authority, while ten days later at Yom HaKippurim, the prayers turn toward pleas of forgiveness. Following Yom HaKippurim, only five days later, Israel enters into Sukkot, the Feast of Tabernacles, to dwell with the Divine Presence. This is the prophetic time of which Zechariah prophesies:

> Then it will come about that any who are left of all the nations that went against Jerusalem will go up from year to year to worship the King, the LORD of hosts, and to celebrate the Feast of Booths.[137]

Zechariah then prophesies something which sounds familiar, a "smiting" and "punishment" once applied to Israel in the wilderness, in effect, expanding the authority of the Angel of the Presence over all the earth:

137. Ze 14:16

> If the family of Egypt does not go
> up or enter, then no rain will fall on
> them; it will be the plague with which
> the LORD *smites the nations* who do
> not go up to celebrate the Feast of
> Booths. *This will be the punishment*
> of Egypt, and the punishment of all
> the nations who do not go up to
> celebrate the Feast of Booths.[138]

The cloud conditions of Israel now extend and bind the nations of the earth under the authority of the Angel of the Presence. The person of Messiah Yeshua, a "man" who calls himself the "Son of man," was given extraordinary authority to forgive sin. He will also rule over the earth with the Divine authority of the Father. After the world has the opportunity to recognize him as having the authority of the King at Rosh HaShanah, and after they have sincerely sought forgiveness, represented by Yom HaKippurim, they will then enter into rewards and punishments during the Feast of Sukkot. Each individual will now have to live with his choices of rebellion or obedience to the commandments.

138. Ze 14:19-20

8

PORTIONS IN THE CLOUD

Behaalotkha **"in your going up"** to light the menorah is in Numbers 8:1-12:16

Ki Tisa **"when you elevate"** to give a ransom for your soul and escape the plague is in Numbers 30:11-34:35

Pekudei records the **"accounting, reckoning"** of the Tabernacle in Numbers 38:21-40:38

The seven-branched menorah is the first subject of the Torah portion Beha'alotkha.[139] In the Tabernacle, the lighting of the seven-branched lamp, or menorah, was accompanied by the burning of incense. It was a "tamid" or perpetual offering, prophesying of something that endures. The incense on the hot coals from the brazen altar created clouds in the tent:

> Moreover, you shall make an altar
> as a place for burning incense...And
> Aaron shall burn fragrant incense
> on it; he shall burn it every morning
> when he trims the lamps. And when
> Aaron *trims the lamps at twilight*, he

139. Nu 8:1-12:16

95

shall burn incense. There shall be
perpetual incense before the LORD
throughout your generations.[140]

The High Priest offered the clouds (prayers) before the
seven lamps. There is a great "cloud" of witnesses.
Traditionally, lay Israelites accompanied the priests
and Levites in their daily service with prayers and
fasting. The priests, Levites, and the lay "watchers"
represented the entire nation of Israel in the service
of the altar. They witnessed and they were witnesses
to the various lessons of salvation, redemption,
sanctification, resurrection, repentance, and
gratefulness represented by the altar sacrifices.

> And I heard the altar saying, 'Yes,
> O Lord God, the Almighty, true and
> righteous are Your judgments.' The
> fourth angel poured out his bowl
> upon the sun, and it was given to it
> to scorch men with fire. Men were
> scorched with fierce heat; *and they*
> *blasphemed the name of God who*
> *has the power over these plagues,*
> *and they did not repent so as to give*
> *Him glory.*[141]

When an altar talks, it's worth listening to the
message. In this case, the altar mentions those who
will blaspheme the Name of God who has power
over plagues. This is an easy connection. The Angel
in the Cloud could exercise judgment over the Book,
and he had the power of forgiveness for sin.

> The LORD said to Moses, 'Whoever
> has sinned against Me, I will blot
> him out of My book. But go now,
> lead the people where I told you.
> Behold, *My angel shall go before*
> *you; nevertheless in the day when I*
> *punish, I will punish them for their sin.'*
> *Then the LORD smote the people,*

140. Ex 30:7-8

141.Re 16:7-9

*because of what they did with the
calf which Aaron had made.*

The angel in the pillar of cloud and fire spoke with Moses. The Angel of the Presence in the pillar of cloud both spoke the Word to Moses and had the authority of the Name within him to pardon or not pardon transgressions of that Word. Significantly, the plague fell on the Israelites who sinned with the Golden Calf.

The men in Revelation who blasphemed the Name were blaspheming the Angel of the Presence who has the power to pardon or not to pardon. Messiah Yeshua is the one with the power over the plagues, but many men in Revelation 16:9 refuse to give him the glory as the believers did in Matthew: "But when the crowds saw this, they were awestruck, and glorified God, who had given such authority to men."[142] In order to glorify Elohim, one must obey and give honor to the Angel of His Presence, Yeshua. To rebel against Yeshua, the Living Word, is to blaspheme the One who sent him to judge human behavior according to the Book. Yeshua was so careful to say that he did not come to abolish one tiny stroke of the Torah, the seed of understanding his and his apostles' apocalyptic Scriptures.

The Torah portion Pekudei means "Accounting of." Pekudei is Exodus 38:21-40:38. Throughout the wilderness journey, Israel was constantly judged as to their fitness to live in the traveling cloud and to be a part of the Tabernacle worship. The Father in Heaven assigned that job to the Angel in the cloud, and those who lived in the cloud were accounted for in the journey. They were reckoned as part of the cloud or not: "For the cloud of the Lord was on the tabernacle by day, and fire was in it by night, in the sight of all the house of Israel throughout all their journeys."[143]

There are significant events in the portion Pekudei:

142. Mt 9:8

143. Ex 40:38

97

- The accounting records of the Mishkan (Tabernacle) building project are established
- the Mishkan is constructed, erected, anointed, and consecrated for service
- the priests are anointed for service
- the glory of Lord fills the Mishkan with the cloud.

The focus of the "Accounting" portion is the clouds of glory and all the construction of the Mishkan, which prophesies of the work of Messiah Yeshua. In the Jewish tradition, the cloud enveloped the camp on their first stop at Sukkot after leaving Egypt, and the Israelites continued living in "clouds of glory" on the journey. This was established previously in Exodus:

> And the LORD was going before them in a pillar of cloud by day to lead them on the way, and in a pillar of fire by night to give them light, that they might travel by day and by night. He did not take away the pillar of cloud by day, nor the pillar of fire by night, from before the people.[144]

The pillar doubled as a cloud holding water by day and fire by night. The height at which the pillar normally positioned itself is unclear, but it could always be seen and it had to descend to ground level to speak with Moses. The portion Ki Tisa describes the descent of the cloud similarly to how it was described at the giving of the Torah at Sinai:

> And the LORD descended in the cloud and stood there with him as he called upon the name of the LORD. Then the LORD passed by in front of him and proclaimed, "The LORD, the LORD God, compassionate and gracious, slow to anger, and

144. Ex 13:21-22

*abounding in lovingkindness and
truth...*[145]

*Then Moses went up to the
mountain, and the cloud covered
the mountain. And the glory of the
LORD rested (shaken) on Mount
Sinai, and the cloud covered it for
six days; and on the seventh day He
called to Moses from the midst of the
cloud. And to the eyes of the sons
of Israel the appearance of the glory
of the LORD was like a consuming
fire on the mountain top. And Moses
entered the midst of the cloud as he
went up to the mountain;*[146]

In the two "descent" passages above, there are
many of the traditional Jewish symbols and idioms
of the Fall feasts: Rosh HaShanah, Yom HaKippurim,
and Sukkot:

- Clouds
- Glory
- Dwelling in the Presence
- Coverings
- Torah

In other words, Sukkot of Glory. Like the example
of the Yarden River that descends, yet on at least
two previous occasions of deliverance and reward,
ascended, so Ki Tisa describes the descent of the
Presence in a cloud, yet it means to "lift up" a
ransom for the soul to be reckoned as part of Israel.
With Yeshua as redeemer, one day the souls of the
righteous will be lifted up into his glory.

Ki Tisa's seeds of the clouds, the Angel of the
Presence, forgiveness, judgment, repentance, and
the elevation of Israel to dwell in the Cloud are grown
into many Jewish traditions concerning the Feast of
Trumpets, Yom HaKippurim, and Sukkot. It's time to

145. Ex 34:5-8

146. Ex 24:15-18

replace words like "rapture" with Scriptural ones like cloud, glory, Presence, dwelling...and "When you elevate..." Even the half-shekel representing Israel's dependence upon one another to make a whole cloud of witnesses is a prophecy.

The three traditional Jewish themes of Rosh HaShanah (and fall feasts) are:

- Kingship: throne/authority
- Remembrance: repentance/judgment
- Shofar: shout/voice

The symbol of the throne is strong in relation to the Feast of Sukkot. The root of *sukkah* is also related to the word *sokek*,[147] which is a covered structure. The cherubim's wings were to cover (*sakak*) the mercy seat, or throne, in the tabernacle[148] and the Temple.[149]

Found in 2 Kings 16:18 is the passage where it describes "the covered way for the sabbath" which was removed by wicked King Ahaz. There is another possible translation of this verse, which is that *shabbat* is to be read as "throne:" King Ahaz removed the "the covered place of the throne" after he removed the precious silver and gold vessels of the Temple, gave them to the king of Assyria, and set another altar, a pagan altar beside the altar of Adonai.

Regardless of how the verse is translated, whether as the covered way for the Sabbath or the covered place of the throne, anyone who tries to remove Israel's cloud covering of Sukkot is in a confederacy with the King of Assyria, a type of antichrist in the Prophets. An anti-christ is one who is against the Messiah, the Living Word. By removing Israel's covering of Sabbath, the anti-Messiah attempts to subvert the throne and Kingdom of Messiah, our rest in Messiah Yeshua. The Sabbath cloud "clothes" us for our dwelling with Messiah Yeshua.

147. Strong's H1492
148. Ex 37:9
149. 1 Ch 28:18

The cloud stood by Moses while Adonai passed by and spoke to him. The voice of Adonai came from the cloud. Moses entered the glory of Adonai in a cloud on the Seventh Day, or symbolically, entered the "rest" of His glory.

> And it came about, whenever Moses entered the tent, the pillar of cloud would descend and stand at the entrance of the tent; and the LORD would speak with Moses. When all the people saw the pillar of cloud standing at the entrance of the tent, all the people would arise and worship, each at the entrance of his tent.[150]

The cloud claimed a position of judgmental authority at the entrance of the Tent of Meeting. Although the cloud was speaking with Moses, each family would arise and worship at the entrance of its own tent, symbolically joining with Moses in acknowledging the judgments and the testimony being spoken. Each person would testify to the authority of the Angel of the Presence within the little mishkan (tabernacle) of his or her own body.

> Then Moses went up to the mountain, and the cloud covered the mountain. And the glory of the LORD rested (*shaken*- to dwell or be with) on Mount Sinai, and the cloud covered it for six days; and on the seventh day He called to Moses from the midst of the cloud. And to the eyes of the sons of Israel the appearance of the glory of the LORD was like a consuming fire on the mountain top. And Moses entered the midst of the cloud as he went up to the mountain;[151]

150. Ex 33:9-10

151. Ex 24:15-18

101

Moses alone entered the cloud on the mountain, but Israel's location was under the cloud.

Jewish tradition recognizes the symbol of the cloud, the symbol that permeates all Israel's feasts, or sukkot of glory. The Jewish prayer book for Rosh HaShanah is a *Machzor*, and it extensively links the clouds of the feasts to the ingathering.[152] The Israelite entered clouds at Passover in the Exodus from Egypt; the clouds enveloped Israel at Shavuot for the giving of the Torah; and the clouds surrounded them in the wilderness journey, culminating in the Feast of Sukkot to bookend "sukkot of glory.[153] Paul describes this tradition:

> For I do not want you to be unaware, brethren, that our fathers were all *under the cloud*, and all passed through the sea; and *all were baptized into Moses in the cloud* and in the sea;[154]

Paul links the Passover passage at the Reed Sea to the cloud over Sinai at Shavuot. Israel was both "under" and "in" the waters of the cloud, and in Acts 2, they were enveloped in fire, the other aspect of Heaven, *shamayim*. Shamayim is water and fire of the Holy Spirit.

A review of the Seed words:

The Lord Himself **descends**.
The dead **ascend**.
The saints **go up** with them.
They meet the Lord **in the cloud together**.
They **dwell** with the Lord forever.
These words are **comfort**ing.

---

152. Zalman, 2003, pp. 189-190

153. Ibid p. 236-237

154. 1 Co 10:1-2

One of the Seed words cited by Paul to the Thessalonians is "comforted." In the wilderness, the

Israelites sinned with the Golden Calf, and they fell under judgment. To reassure Moses, Adonai descends in the pillar of cloud and recites a Name that contains His attributes of mercy toward the sinner to comfort them.

> And the LORD descended in the
> cloud and stood there with him as he
> called upon the name of the LORD.
> Then the LORD passed by in front
> of him and proclaimed, 'The LORD,
> the LORD God, compassionate
> and gracious, slow to anger, and
> abounding in lovingkindness and
> truth...'[155]

The watery and fiery cloud was the focal point of gathering the community, encouraging the community to move, and comforting the community. Yeshua, like the cloud, also gathers and comforts:

> *Gathering them together,* He
> commanded them not to leave
> Jerusalem, but to wait for what the
> Father had promised, 'Which,' He
> said, 'you heard of from Me; for John
> *baptized with water,* but *you will
> be baptized with the Holy Spirit* not
> many days from now.'[156]

The Holy Spirit is the Comforter to those who gathered Israel after their dismal failure at Mount Sinai. They'd received the Torah and broken it within 40 days. They were comforted with the assurance of mercy in the cloud. On an anniversary of the original giving of the Torah at Sinai (Shavuot/Pentecost), Yeshua tells his disciples to gather again to be comforted and taught the Word:

> But the Comforter, which is the Holy
> Ghost, whom the Father will send
> in my name, he shall teach you all

155. Ex 34:5-8

156. Ac 1:5

103

> things, and bring all things to your
> remembrance, whatsoever I have
> said unto you.[157]

> When the day of Pentecost had
> come, they were all together in one
> place.[158]

This Comforter would enable them to learn the Word and keep it. It would enable them to gather even more people than just the direct descendants of Abraham. This long-distance gathering would be a sign of the Kingdom, paving the way for the ingathering into the clouds of glory when Yeshua returned.

> So *when they had come together*,
> they were asking Him, saying, 'Lord,
> is it at this time You are restoring the
> kingdom[159] to Israel?' He said to
> them, 'It is not for you to know times
> or epochs which the Father has fixed
> by His own authority; but you will
> receive power when the Holy Spirit
> has come upon you; and you shall
> be My witnesses both in Jerusalem,
> and in all Judea and Samaria, and
> even to the remotest part of the
> earth.'[160]

157. Jn 14:26 (KJV)

158. Ac 2:1

159. Kingdom, royal authority, the Heavenly Throne, and the crown are all traditional Jewish symbols of the fall feasts: Trumpets, Atonement, and Tabernacles.

This coming together was the first step toward a worldwide scattering to prepare the righteous for a greater gathering, an ingathering into Sukkot of Glory. After Yeshua delivers this message, he then ascends into the cloud.

> And after He had said these things,
> *He was lifted up* while they were
> looking on, and *a cloud received
> Him* out of their sight.

160. Ac 1:6-8

So the disciples will understand that the wilderness

104

cloud of glory was the pattern, two angels assure them that just as the wilderness cloud ascended and descended to lead, comfort, and gather all Israel, so would Yeshua return just as he always did:

> And as they were gazing intently into the sky while He was going, behold, two men in white clothing stood beside them. They also said, 'Men of Galilee, why do you stand looking into the sky? This Jesus, who has been *taken up from you into heaven, will come in just the same way* as you have watched Him go into heaven.'[161]

Read the text carefully, and it doesn't say that Yeshua grew smaller and smaller until he disappeared into space. He simply lifted up and a cloud received him. The cloud is not so far away.

Yeshua taught his disciples to immerse new believers in the Name. The Name of the Father, the Son, and the Holy Spirit are the same, for the Name is in the Son:

> But the eleven disciples proceeded to Galilee, to the mountain which Jesus had designated. When they saw Him, they worshiped Him; but some were doubtful. And Jesus came up and spoke to them, saying, 'All authority has been given to Me in heaven and on earth. Go therefore and make disciples of all the nations, baptizing them in the name of the Father and the Son and the Holy Spirit, teaching them to observe all that I commanded you; and lo, I am with you always, even to the end of the age.'[162]

161. Ac 1:4–11

162. Mt 28:16-20

In I Thessalonians 4:16-18, Paul also writes concerning a cloud immersion that causes the believers to ascend rather than go down into the watery cloud:

> For the Lord Himself will descend
> from heaven with a shout, with
> the voice of the archangel and
> with the trumpet of God, and the
> dead in Christ will rise first. Then we
> who are alive and remain will be
> caught up together with them in
> the clouds to meet the Lord in the
> air, and so we shall always be with
> the Lord. Therefore, comfort one
> another with these words.

In this explanation, the Lord Himself descends from Heaven with a shout, but the saints are caught up. Where are they going? Where is "up"? With a little investigation into the Greek word for "air," it doesn't seem as though the air to which the saints are gathered is that high up. In fact, from the definition, one could infer that it is possible to respire normally:

> Strong's #109 aer from aemi (to
> breathe unconsciously, i.e. respire;
> by analogy, to blow)
>
> Definition: the air, particularly the
> lower and denser air as distinguished
> from the higher and rarer air

The phrase that is translated into English as "caught up" is likely translated to match the idea of "air" as the place of gathering, but the Greek word simply means to seize or snatch away, not up. Perhaps the clouds are a little lower to the ground at this future Feast of Trumpets than the English translation implies.

Paul's explanation of the cloud as a mikveh (baptism) describes an immersion into both fire and water. Israel received the Torah under the cloud over the fiery mountain at Shavuot, and they were symbolically immersed in water and fire. Yeshua's disciples were also immersed in Shavuot fire, and the new disciples were immediately immersed in water.

Moses is a metaphor for Torah, just as The House is a metaphor for the Temple or Heaven is a euphemism and metaphor for Adonai. Both fiery cloud and sea contain mikveh water, so when we mikveh, or immerse ourselves into Messiah, we establish the Torah and Messiah Yeshua as the cloud of Adonai's Presence; now He now dwells, or *shokhen*, in us at Shavuot. It is immersion into the Word of God and the Testimony of Yeshua as that Word.

50,000 DEGREES

A bit of Jewish tradition gives a very specific hint as to the place of Yeshua's return by distance from Jerusalem. Yeshua's return is only a Sabbath day's journey from Jerusalem. A Sabbath-day's journey[163] is a distance of 2,000 cubits, or less than half-a-mile, the distance to which, according to Jewish tradition, it was allowable to travel on the Sabbath day without violating the law.[164] Modern Jewish application is that maximum walking range from one's city is 2,000 cubits (0.596 miles).

However, this measurement starts 70 2/3 cubits from the city limits. Practically speaking, this means that you may not walk a straight line more than .598 miles in any direction in the unpopulated area outside your city limits. The application, or halakha, considers all contiguous housing to be part of the same city. It would be permitted to walk hundreds of miles from city to city if the whole way was populated. The Mount of Olives is within this limit.

> For just as the lightning comes from the east, and flashes even to the west, so shall the coming of the Son of Man be. Wherever the corpse

163. Ac 1:12; Ex 16:29; Nu 35:5; Jo 3:4

164. *Eastman's Bible Dictionary*, 1897

is, there the vultures will gather. But
immediately after the tribulation of
those days the sun will be darkened,
and the moon will not give its light,
and the stars will fall from the sky,
and the powers of the heavens will
be shaken, and then the sign of the
Son of Man will appear in the sky,
and then all the tribes of the earth
will mourn, and they will see the Son
of Man coming on the clouds of the
sky with power and great glory. And
He will send forth His   angels with a
great trumpet[165] and they will gather
together His elect from the four
winds, from one end of the sky to the
other.[166]

And I looked, and behold, a white
cloud, and sitting on the cloud was
one like a son of man, having a
golden crown on His head, and a
sharp sickle in His hand. And another
angel came out of the temple,
crying out with a loud voice to Him
who sat on the cloud, 'Put in your
sickle and reap, because the hour to
reap has come, because the harvest
of the earth is ripe.'[167]

If the two witnesses of Revelation correspond to
the two witnesses speaking with Yeshua at the
transfiguration, Moses and Elijah, then they also will
return to the earth before being killed, resurrected,
and once again caught up in the cloud. The cloud
also receives the two resurrected witnesses:

165. Yom Kippur

166. Mt 24:27-31

167. Re 14:14-16

And they heard a loud voice from
heaven saying to them, 'Come up
here.' And they went up into heaven
in the cloud, and their enemies
beheld them. And in that hour

there was a great earthquake, and
a tenth of the city fell; and seven
thousand people were killed in
the earthquake, and the rest were
terrified and gave glory to the God
of heaven.[168]

The role of the two witnesses is to point to the Angel
of the Presence in whom is the most sacred Name of
Adonai. Refusing to obey Him is blasphemy. Those
who do not want to acknowledge Yeshua as the
Angel of the Presence in the cloud will be glad when
these two witnesses appear to have been killed.
The tribes of the earth do not want to acknowledge
Yeshua as the Messiah for many reasons; likewise,
the tribes of the earth do not want to acknowledge
that Elijah and Moses spoke in harmony with Yeshua;
in fact, their words of prophecy were his, for he was
the prophecy.

As with the pillar of cloud in the wilderness, the cloud
that calls up the resurrected witnesses hovers above
the earth, not at ground level. This cloud of fire
and water is a little hard to pin down! It ascends,
descends, moves, speaks, and transforms in its
protection and judgment.

In *Ki Tisa*, those who lacked the quality of repentance
were those who "did not repent so as to give Him
glory."[169] The difference between those afflicted with
the plagues and those who were spared from the
great Jerusalem earthquake was that those who
were spared *did* give "glory to the God of heaven."
When Yeshua sends his angels with the great trumpet
of Yom HaKippurim to gather his elect, the Matthew
text says that he returns with power and "great
glory." Either this is the glory of the Living Holy One of
Israel, or it is not.

If it is not, then we could expect this imposter or
usurper to suffer the same plagues and judgments
as those who refused to give glory to God. The

168. Re 11:12-13

169. Re 16:7-9

111

only conclusion is that the Son of Man coming on the clouds IS the manifest glory of God, and he is no imposter or rebel, but the Angel of the Presence. Those who acknowledge him as the glory of God will be spared; those who will not repent and obey the Angel of the Presence in order to give glory to God will not.

The cloud is often accompanied by thunder and lightning or shofars, representing the spoken Word or voice of Adonai.

> And he said, 'The LORD came from Sinai, and dawned on them from Seir; He shone forth from Mount Paran, and He came from the midst of ten thousand holy ones; at His right hand there was flashing lightning for them. Indeed, He loves the people; All Your holy ones are in Your hand, and they followed in Your steps; everyone receives of Your words.'[170]

Developing the Right Hand as a symbol of Yeshua as well, the lightning at the right hand contained Adonai's words to a holy people in the person of Yeshua. Those who receive the Word repent, and at Yom HaKippurim, they are gathered into the hand of protection in the cloud, for they have fed from the living, fiery manna of the Torah in that hand. They have fed on the Living Manna that IS the hand. In fact, the NJKV expresses it thus: "From His right hand came a fiery law for them." The one who is the Right Hand of the Father holds the holy ones in his hand because his hand is the Father's hand. They are one and the same! The faithful are placed in Yeshua's hand to hear the voice of the Word:

> My sheep hear My voice, and I know them, and they follow Me; and I give eternal life to them, and they

170. Dt 33:2-3

shall never perish; and no one shall
snatch them out of My hand.

My Father, who has given *them* to
Me, is greater than all; and no one
is able to snatch *them* out of the
Father's hand. I and the Father are
one."[171]

Ever try to snatch M&Ms from someone else's hand
as a game when you were young? If you were fast
enough to snatch the M&M, it was yours. If Yeshua's
movement is as fast as lightning, then his holy ones
have nothing to fear. There is no enemy dead or
alive that is fast enough to snatch Yeshua's sheep or
an M&M out of his hand.

White Lightning

What is the glorified Yeshua's appearance like? It
can take many forms, but to Daniel, he appears like
lightning:

I lifted my eyes and looked, and
behold, there was a certain man
dressed in linen, whose waist was
girded with *a belt of* pure gold of
Uphaz. His body also was like beryl,
his face had the appearance of
lightning, his eyes were like flaming
torches, his arms and feet like the
gleam of polished bronze, and the
sound of his words like the sound of a
tumult (roar).[172]

The words of Yeshua sound like a tumult, or a roar.
This tumult can be traced back to the Creation:

It is He who made the earth by
His power, Who established the
world by His wisdom, And by His
understanding He stretched out the

171. Jo 10:27-30

172. Da 10:5-6

113

heavens. When He utters His voice,
there is a tumult of waters in the
heavens, and He causes the clouds
to ascend from the end of the earth;
He makes lightning for the rain,
and brings forth the wind from His
storehouses.[173]

The voice of God, and therefore the voice of Yeshua, is often equated to the sound of thunder, but it is also described by Jeremiah as a tumult of waters that causes clouds to form accompanied by lightning. Yeshua is the voice of God, and his voice is as the voice of many waters. Job describes the voice of Adonai with accompanying thunder:

At this also my heart trembles, and
leaps from its place. Listen closely
to the thunder of His voice, and
the rumbling that goes out from His
mouth. Under the whole heaven
He lets it loose, and His lightning
to the ends of the earth. After it,
a voice roars; He thunders with His
majestic voice; and He does not
restrain the lightnings when His voice
is heard. God thunders with His
voice wondrously, doing great things
which we cannot comprehend.[174]

Lightning accompanies the voice of Adonai, which is only right considering Yeshua's glorified body is like lightning.

A single lightning "flash" is formed by a series of lightning "strokes." Usually there are about four strokes per flash. The number 4 is represented in Hebrew by the letter ד *delet*. It is *dalet*, the door, which alludes to Yeshua as the opening and authority through which the Earth connects to the Heavens: "So Jesus said to them again, 'Truly, truly, I say to you, I am the door of the sheep...I am the door; if anyone enters

173. Je 51:15-16

174. Job 37:1-5

114

through Me, he will be saved, and will go in and out and find pasture.'"[175] The physical lightning door connects the heavens to the earth in a trajectory so fast that it can heat to 50,000 degrees F.!

Lightning is attracted to tall, "proud" objects on the earth. High places are to be avoided during a thunderstorm. Experts recommend prostrating yourself on the ground if you feel your hair become prickly! Not a bad idea if you hear the voice of Yeshua, either.

Red Sprites

The stones set in the breastplate of the High Priest in the Torah portion Pekudei are significant. Even the precious stones in Aaron's Breastplate of Judgment are said to have been carried to the wilderness by a cloud along with the manna![176]

The Red Sprites that appear over a thunderstorm may have a connection to those stones. A sprite means a spirit. Red Sprites are massive luminous flashes that appear directly above an active thunderstorm. They occur at the same time as cloud-to-ground or intracloud lightning strokes. The structure of a sprite can be small single or multiple vertically elongated spots. Sprites are most often red and usually occur in pairs of two or more.

What do red sprites in a thunderstorm have to do with the throne of Heaven that thunders and lightnings the Word of Adonai? Here is what John describes once he had been transported through the door opening of Heaven:

> At once I was in the Spirit, and
> there before me was a throne in
> heaven with someone sitting on
> it. And the one who sat there had
> the appearance of jasper and
> carnelian.[177]

175. Jn 10:7,9

176. Biderman, 2011, p. 262

177. Re 4:2-3

Jasper in Hebrew is *yashpheh*, meaning, "glittering." Jasper is the last of the gems in the high priest's breastplate. It is first of New Jerusalem's foundations. Jasper is usually a shade of red in color. It can be highly polished and is used for seals. When the colors are in stripes or bands, it is called *striped* or *banded* jasper. This is similar to the vertical bands in red sprites.

The second stone describing the One on the throne is carnelian, a red or reddish-brown stone. The word is derived from the Latin word meaning flesh, in reference to the flesh color sometimes exhibited. If Red Sprites occur in pairs, might they reflect the appearance of the One on the throne whose appearance is both in brightness of both spirit and the flesh?

Blue Jets

Blue jets are a second set of phenomena that appear above thunderstorms. These are narrow cones that are ejected from the electrically active core regions of a thunderstorm. According to the Merriam-Webster, a jet may be "a narrow stream of material emanating or appearing to emanate from a celestial object." To what celestial object could the blue jets testify?

> Then Moses went up with Aaron,
> Nadab and Abihu, and seventy of
> the elders of Israel, and they saw
> the God of Israel; and under His feet
> there appeared to be a pavement
> of sapphire, as clear as the sky
> itself.[178]

These thunderstorm colors correspond to the red of jasper and carnelian, the appearance of the One who sits on the throne; the blue jets are the color of the sapphire pavement under His feet. After the jasper, the sapphire is the second foundation stone of New Jerusalem. The earth does declare the glory

178. Ex 24:9-10

116

of the Heavens. Yeshua's holy ones do declare and give glory to Elohim, and they obey the Angel of His Presence in the Temples of their bodies on earth. Those who will be gathered to New Jerusalem will find 50,000 degrees and cloudy to be quite comfortable, thank you.

10

THE RED SHADOW

This chapter originally appeared in the BEKY Book *Truth, Tradition, or Tare: Growing in the Word*. It is included in this booklet as a bonus chapter for the sake of context and continuity, and additional material augments the theme of *Clouds of Glory*.

The Torah holds the Seed words from which the rest of the Older Testament (TANAKH) and Newer Testament grow. Those books of Scripture between Joshua and Revelation document traditions grown from the Torah. In fact, even the Torah seeds the idea that customs will grow from the Torah itself:

> Therefore, to this day the sons of
> Israel do not eat the sinew of the hip
> which is on the *socket* of the thigh,
> because he touched the socket
> of Jacob's thigh in the sinew of the
> hip.[179]

This ancient battle between Esau and Jacob is a Seed pattern demonstrating both the struggle of mankind and the practice of traditions to preserve the memory of a Seed event in the Torah.

The sensitive areas of both the foot and the hand

179. Ge 32:32

119

are symbolic in Scripture. The foot, specifically the heel, represents the soul. In Hebrew, the soul is the *nefesh*. The shortest definition of the soul is a bundle of appetites, emotions, desires, and intellect. The heel becomes very hard and calloused, but the sole (Hebrew: *kaph*) remains highly sensitive. When Jacob is born, he is holding onto red, hairy Esau's heel, pointing to the place of Esau's vulnerability, his appetites. The heel is the point of vulnerability to Eve's "seed," yet the point of vulnerability to the serpent-beast is the head, the symbol of the spirit.

In his appetite for the "red stuff" and Canaanite women, Esau is both hardened predator and vulnerable prey, like a beast. He hunts for game and that which pleases his soul, and this is exactly how Jacob deceives his father Isaac out of Esau's blessing and bargains with Esau for his birthright in Genesis 25. His soul appetites were what made Esau the prey, for all that is needed to bait a Red One like Esau is food, the hunt (competition), sexual pleasure, emotional pleasure, or intellectual achievement. Being governed by these desires instead of mastering them with the Spirit are the beast's vulnerabilities.

Esau[180] represents the red stuff, a rowdy soul seeking pleasure and achievement. When Jacob returns to the Land to face Esau, he struggles one night with a "man," whom he declares has the face of God, and Jacob names the place of the wrestling match Peniel. This struggle resulted in Jacob being smitten in the thigh socket, the *caph*[181].

Before Jacob could face his twin Esau, he had to wrestle the Esau within. Jacob[182] was notorious for relying on his own heel, which in Jacob's case, was the hardened intellect of his soul, to obtain the result he wanted. Jacob, too, needed for his spirit to prevail over his red soul in order to conquer Red One within, for this is a competition worth winning. It changed Jacob's walk to do so, as it will any disciple's walk when he practices walking after the Spirit instead of

180. Esau's nickname in Scripture is Edom, the Red One, from *adom*, which means red in Hebrew.

181. *Caph* in Hebrew denotes things with a cup-like structure, like the palm of the hand, the sole of the foot, or the thigh socket. The Jewish male headcover is called a *kippah*, for its cuplike structure resembles the cupping of a hand on the head to ordain, bless, or consecrate. *Caphar* means atonement, from which come the word for the appointed time of Yom Kippur, the Day of Atonement. Leviticus 14:18 is a good example of the overlapping themes of caph and caphar.

his soul. When a disciple walks in the Spirit, it is with the sensitivity of the sole of his foot to the Spirit, not the vulnerability to his red desires.[183]

In Revelation Three, the fifth assembly is Sardis. It literally means "Red Ones." In rabbinic tradition, Esau (Edom) is the Red One, for he was born red and hairy all over like a beast, and Esau's Biblical nickname Edom comes from *adom*, or the color red. The Sardinians are singled out as conforming to the image of the hairy beast Esau, a man controlled by his appetites. The Seed of the Torah hints to the principle of the first born beast, for in Day Six of Creation, the beast was created first, yet the second-born man was created to rule over the beasts, for the man was made in the image of Elohim, who is Spirit.

When he walks into to his father's tent not knowing that Jacob has already deceived his way to the blessing, Esau tells his father, "I am your *firstborn*, Esau." Because his father Isaac has been deceived through his own red soul, his vulnerable appetite for wild game, the Red One Esau is right on target. Isaac began his walk with the God of his father Abraham by sowing seed in the field and reaping a hundredfold, yet at a critical time of rendering the blessing to the firstborn, Isaac is vulnerable to the appetites of a man who hunts in the field instead of sowing seed in it! These are critical links between the serpent, the most cunning beast of the field (Gen. 3:1) and the man of the field, Esau (Gen. 25:27).

Each of the seven assemblies in the Book of Revelation correspond to a *moed*, or feast day, listed in the Torah.[184] The assembly at Sardis is the easiest example of the seven, for several phrases, idioms, and traditions relative to Rosh HaShanah, the Feast of Trumpets, establish that Yeshua's message to Sardis is almost word-for-word a collection of Jewish tradition on the feast. Were all those Jewish traditions gleaned from the scarce Seeds in the Torah?

182. Jacob in Hebrew is Yaakov, commonly translated as "supplanter," but the root ekev refers to the heel or that which comes after.

183. For a thorough study into the spirit, soul, body, and the Esau/Jacob symbols, see the author's *Creation Gospel Workbook Four: The Scarlet Harlot and the Crimson Thread*.

184. See *Creation Gospel Workbook One: The Creation Foundation* for a complete explanation of the Seven Churches of Revelation as the Seven Feasts of Adonai listed in the Torah. For an easy reference, see Appendix A.

While there may be some Jewish traditions of uncertain origin, the Scriptures uphold the traditions of Rosh HaShanah in Revelation, so we can be sure they're grown from good Seed, and if the Red Ones are willing to repent of their poor motivations, then fruit will grow from good soil, a clean heart, good fruit from good Seed.

Rosh HaShanah initiates the Fall season of feasts in the Torah. Examine each statement from Revelation 3:1-6 addressed to the Red Ones below, and a shadow Seed from the Torah explains from where the Jewish tradition may have grown.

> To the angel of the church in Sardis write: He who has *the seven Spirits of God* and the *seven stars*, says this: 'I know your deeds, that you have a name that you are *alive, but you are dead.*'

Torah Seed: A traditional Jewish Torah portion begins in Numbers 8:1 with the seven-branched menorah, representing the Seven Spirits of God and the seven assemblies. The [chiastic] middle of the seven days of Creation is the fourth, the day when the stars were placed to witness to the *moedim*[185] (feasts).

Jewish tradition: Deeds are examined each year from Rosh HaShanah to Yom HaKippur. Figuratively, the dead one resurrects from the deeds of the past year in order to navigate the path that the Father has decreed for him in the coming year. As he hears the sound of the shofar[186]/ trumpet on Rosh HaShanah, the repentant one dies (sleeps) and is resurrected "in the twinkling of an eye." This is exactly what Paul teaches his Gentile converts:

> Behold, I tell you a mystery; we will not all sleep, but we will all

185. Ge 1:14

186. ram's horn blown like a trumpet

be changed, in a moment, in the twinkling of an eye, at the last trumpet; for the trumpet will sound, and the dead will be raised imperishable, and we will be changed.[187]

The "last trump" is the trumpet of Rosh HaShanah, and the "great trump" is sounded ten days later at Yom Kippur.

The pillar of cloud arose for travel in the wilderness, guiding the Israelites along the pre-determined path. The pattern of rising is one theme embedded in Jewish Rosh HaShanah tradition of the greater resurrection from the dead. Significantly, the Sardinians are told to "Wake up, and strengthen the things that remain, which were about to die; for I have not found your deeds completed in the sight of My God." Jewish tradition connects the deeds of the past and the coming years with repentance, death, and resurrection:

> A widespread Ashkenazic practice is for men to wear a white cloak called a kittel on Yom Kippur. Sefer Ra'avyah (no. 528) explains that on Yom Kippur, we resemble angels. Wearing a kittel reflects our spiritual purity in this elevated state. Rema (Shulchan Arukh, Orah Hayyim 610:4), on the other hand, avers that the kittel resembles *a shroud. The image of death should jolt one into repentance.*[188]

Torah Seed: The act of waving the offering in Numbers Eight is an "elevation"[189] that shadows resurrection from something old to something new. The Levites even shaved all their body hair before their elevation, symbolically returning to a newborn state and immersing in water

187. 1 Co 15:51–52

188. Angel, 2000, p. 43

189. You can hear the root of *alah*, for "going up" (Strong's #5927) in the title of the Torah portion *Beha**alot**kha* (Numbers 8:1-12:16); it means to ascend, to climb, or to sprout forth like vegetation. The menorah was crafted with almond blossoms, demonstrating the Ruach's (Holy Spirit's) resurrection power.

like a womb for their dedication to service in the House.

Jewish tradition: The completion of each year's circuit is the time to examine one's self for success or failure in navigating the prescribed path. As the person has aged through the year, he dies and is resurrected on Rosh HaShanah. The good lives on, but the Red One's transgressions should die as the believer confesses his sins[190]. A common saying at Rosh HaShanah is "Awake you sleeper, arise from the dead." In the words of the Rambam[191], the shofar calls out, "Awaken you sleepers from your (spiritual) slumber. Search out your ways and return to Hashem [God] in Teshuva [repentance]."

This resurrection tradition of the Fifth Feast, the Feast of Trumpets/Rosh HaShanah, is chiastic[192] to the Third Feast, Firstfruits of the Barley, and Firstfruits is also a resurrection day, coinciding with the day that Yeshua and the righteous saints of old resurrected from the dead.[193] Telling the Red Ones of the Fifth Church to "strengthen the things that remain" is a hint to the Fifth Spirit of Adonai, Gvurah, or Strength.

On the Fifth Day of Creation, Elohim creates the birds and fish. In the prophetic shadow of the Torah portion Seed, the rabble reject the manna and crave free fish like they had in Egypt, and Adonai gives them birds to eat until they come out of their noses. Moses is skeptical, asking if all the fish of the sea were gathered, would it be enough? The Israelites complained of the manna that "parched" their souls, but the chiastic resurrection-mate of Sardis is Pergamum, which is promised "hidden manna"[194] if they overcome their parched souls with what the Spirit said. If Israel's flesh and soul appetites could be ruled by spiritual appetites, then resurrection could occur as the Bread of Life taught.

Numbers 11:7-9 gives contextual clues linked to

190. 1 Jo 1:9

191. Maimonides, a respected Jewish scholar

192. A chiasm occurs when two sides become a mirror of the other. If the menorah were folded at its middle, then the third and fifth days would touch; since both emerge from the same "bud" location on the central trunk of the menorah, they share the same theme, resurrection.

193. Mt 27:53

194. Yeshua identifies himself as the Bread from Heaven, identifying both as the manna hidden with the commandments in the Ark of the Covenant and the Word hidden with the Father until he was sent to feed Israel.

Yeshua's admonition to his disciples in Matthew 24:40-41 concerning those "taken" and those "left." Yeshua says,

> Then there will be two men *in the field*; one is[195] taken and one will be left.
>
> Two women will be *grinding at the mill*; one is taken and one will be left.

The First Mention of "grinding" (with a mill) is found in Exodus[196] when Moses ground to powder the gold of the Golden Calf. The second mention, however, in Numbers 11 has a subtle clue to both the First Mention as well as an earlier text describing Eden:

> Now the *manna* was like coriander seed, and its appearance like that of *bdellium*. The people would go about and gather *it* and *grind it between two millstones* or beat *it* in the mortar, and boil *it* in the pot and make cakes with it; and its taste was as the taste of cakes baked with oil. When the dew fell on the camp at night, the manna would fall with it.

In the first verses of the Song of Moses, a song still sung by the holy ones in Revelation, the sent one Moses likens the Word of God to dew on thirsty grass:

> Give ear, O heavens, and let me speak; and let the earth hear the words of my mouth.
>
> Let my teaching[197] drop as the rain, my speech distill as the dew, as the droplets on the fresh grass.[198]

The thirsty green grass soaks up the dew just as those who inhabit heavens and earth are to soak up the

195. In the NASB, the translation is "will be taken," but the annotation is that the literal text reads "is" in both examples.

196. Ex 32:20

197. The Hebrew word for "teaching" (Strong's #3948) is *likach*, a derivative of *lakach*, the Hebrew word for "taken." *Lakach* (Strong's #3947) is used in the sense of taking a wife or acquiring something for a relationship. *Likach* means a *learning*, *teaching*: instruction (1), learning (2), persuasions (1), persuasive -ness (2), teaching (3).

198. Dt 32:1-2

teaching of Adonai as it distills into food like manna. This manna, however, cannot be absorbed merely as physical sustenance; it must be absorbed and digested as the Bread of Heaven, a spiritual food for the spirit of man.

The manna's appearance was like bdellium, a precious stone that acted as a prism for light just as the dew acts as a prism for the morning sun, refracting the light of Heaven's teaching from the Throne that is surrounded by the rainbow of the Seven Spirits of Adonai into the seven colors of the rainbow seen on Earth. The women ground the manna for consumption, but the challenge posed by Yeshua is whether each "woman" grinding the Word sees it as merely physical bread which does not satisfy, or whether she grinds cheerfully the living food from Heaven.

Righteous women in Scripture often symbolize the Holy Spirit[199], and this woman "grinds" spiritual bread with a hearing, cheerful heart. The manna had the appearance of bdellium, the precious stones found in a place of Eden called Havilah where there is "Good Gold." The rabbinic understanding of the grammatical structure of Good Gold in Hebrew is that it is not a description of metal resources in Eden, but of a proper name: Good Gold.

199. For a complete study on the matriarchs of Scripture functioning as parables of the Holy Spirit, see *Creation Gospel Workbook Four: The Scarlet Harlot and the Crimson Thread* by the author.

Who is this Good Gold living in the land of Havilah in Eden? Perhaps it is those who are empowered of the Holy Spirit in the World to Come, a people feasting on the precious bdellium, manna from Heaven. Yeshua is the Manna of Heaven who reveals the precious Holy Spirit from the Father with his speech, and he feeds those who cheerfully receive his teaching, which is how he "takes" his Bride in intimate relationship. The moisture of cleansing water is inherent in the cloud in the wilderness, and to be taken in the cloud is to come into a holy, intimate relationship with Yeshua, the Word of the Father.

Wicked women are parables in Scripture appealing only to a man's lust for physical, emotional, and intellectual satisfaction, and when they grind the Word, there is no regeneration of the Spirit, which leads to more cravings for the meat of the "fleshpots," fish, cucumbers, and leeks of Egypt. Jude cautions against adopting this attitude toward the commandments of Moses:

> These are the men who are hidden
> reefs in your love feasts when they
> feast with you without fear, caring
> for themselves; clouds without water,
> carried along by winds; autumn trees
> without fruit, doubly dead, uprooted;
> wild waves of the sea, casting
> up their own shame like foam;
> wandering stars, for whom the black
> darkness has been reserved forever.
> (12-13)

Those who grind like this woman parable may even obey the commandments, grinding out the understanding of the Word, yet because it is not embraced with the power of the Holy Spirit, the great message of the commandment is lost, which is love toward one's neighbor in addition to the Holy One. The commandment is mercy, justice, and faithfulness to the Spirit of the Torah. These men attend Passover, Shavuot, and Sukkot celebrations only for the sake of themselves. Perhaps they want to dictate the "correct" way to conduct the services; perhaps they want others to notice them; perhaps they merely want to do the commandment in order to be "safe." They reduce the Heavenly Bread to lust for approval and self-righteousness, good feelings, and security.

Jude describes them:

> But these men revile the things
> which they do not understand;
> and the things which they know by

instinct, like unreasoning animals,
by these things they are destroyed.
Woe to them! For they have gone
the way of Cain, and for pay they
have rushed headlong into the
error of Balaam, and perished in the
rebellion of Korah. (10-11)

Jude cites three examples, Cain, Balaam, and Korach, or "the way," "the error," and "the rebellion." Cain sinned by holding back his firstfruits "at the end of days"[200] from both Elohim and his brother Abel. He was selfish and became a hidden reef at the feast of Sukkot, for he was not a cheerful giver or grinder. Balaam sinned by leading the Israelite men into the sins of lust and idolatry, enticing them with Moabite and Midianite women to worship their idols in both eating a meal to those gods and performing acts of sexual lust, which is error in worship. Do we only worship when it "feels" good, or when it is established by "It is written..."?

Korach and his rebels craved spiritual authority that was not theirs. They lusted after the respect, position, and admiration of others, which is spiritual rebellion. These three examples sum up one class of grinders of the Word and distinguish them from those who grind with cheerfulness, for those who thirstily and hungrily receive the Word are not "...grumblers, finding fault, following after their own lusts; they speak arrogantly, flattering people for the sake of gaining an advantage."

200. See *Creation Gospel Workbook Five Vol. I, Torah Portion Miketz,* for an explanation of Cain and Abel's bringing of firstfruits at the End of Days.

201. Dt 34:7

These are examples of the two "women" grinding at the mill. One woman is a Good Gold believer empowered of the Holy Spirit to receive and cheerfully walk in the Word to benefit others. Good Gold has been refined by fire and her walk in the wilderness. She has not become embittered by the hardships and she is still "moist," just as Moses, who, when he died, "his eye was not dim, nor his vigor abated."[201] The Hebrew word for "vigor" is *le-ach,*

128

which means moisture, greenness. Even though it was time for Moses to leave the Earth, the Word from Heaven in the wilderness kept him moist, fresh, and green! Moses knew how to cheerfully "grind" the manna, didn't he?

The other is the woman who strays in her walk, begrudging that which she is taught to share with others, errs in thinking that spiritual life is based on good feelings, and rebels against those placed in positions of spiritual authority or commandeers the tasks assigned to fellow believers. This woman, like the Harlot in Revelation, commits abominations, as Jude warns, flattering for personal advantage. Her gold is not good, for it is formed in error, a waterless cloud, a doubly dead and fruitless tree.

This unrefined gold will be ground to powder and mixed in water, and she will be stripped of her jewelry, forced to drink the cup of adulterous woman, and suffer plague.[202] As Jude points out, those characterized by this grinding woman are ruled by their instincts, beasts that will be destroyed by the very things they crave, and their names will disappear from the Book. Yeshua's same teaching of Heaven that kept Moses moist and green dries these grinders to powder.

Yeshua gave another example, two men in a field. Again, First Mention is a key, and Progressive Mention unfolds the theme. A field functions like two grinders: it offers contrast in how the Word is handled by human beings. They either will conform to the image of the beast like Adam and Eve conformed to the image of the serpent, the most cunning beast of the field, or they will conform to the image of Elohim like Isaac, who sowed and meditated in the field and reaped a hundredfold. The man in the field is the comparable example of the woman at the mill. For more details on the male and female parallels in Scripture, see BEKY Book *Cave of the Couples* by the author.

202. Ex 32-33; Nu 5; Re 17, 9, 16, 18

Jude, which prepares the reader for the final book of the Bible, Revelation, describes those who choose the image of the beast: "…by instinct, like unreasoning animals, by these things they are destroyed." The field can be a place where the Word is sown and produces fruit, a place of prayer and meditation where one walks with Elohim in the cool of the evening like Isaac, or it can be a place of hunting and bloodshed like Esau and Cain's killing fields. Esau, which is Edom, The Red One, shadows the appearance of the scarlet beast allied with the Harlot in Revelation. In like manner, Yeshua presents his disciples with the same choices. What kind of grinder will I be? What will I do in the field?

The Good Gold Man sows, reaps, and gathers the spiritual and physical Seed of the Word, and the Good Gold Woman grinds it cheerfully and feeds the Household of Faith with mercy, justice, and faithfulness.

> So *remember* what you have
> received and heard; and keep it,
> and repent. Therefore if you do not
> wake up, I will come like a thief, and
> *you will not know at what hour I will*
> *come to you.*

 Torah Seed: Rosh HaShanah is a *moed* of remembrance, as detailed in the Seed Torah portion:

> On a day of your gladness, on your festivals, and your new moons, *you shall sound the trumpets* over your *elevation-offerings* and over your peace-offerings; and *they shall be a remembrance* for you before your God. (10:10)

The blasts are associated specifically with *olah* (elevation) offerings of resurrection and the beginning of the months; Rosh HaShanah is a double celebration, for it is both the first of the month, the turn of the year, and the Day of Blowing. Although many think the traditional Jewish nickname for the Feast of Trumpets, Rosh HaShanah, is a misnomer because it is not called by this name specifically in the Torah, there is a textual link to its function.

Rosh HaShanah[203] means "Head (Beginning) of the Year" in Hebrew, but the Torah Seed calls it Yom Teruah, the Day of Blowing [the trumpets]. At first glance, this supplants the Seed with a tare, but does it? *Shanah* in Hebrew is more than a year; it is a change. A year marks a change, so it is a play-on words that Paul renders for his non-Jewish readers to understand:

> Behold, I tell you a mystery; we
> will not all sleep, but *we will all
> be changed*, in a moment, in
> the twinkling of an eye, at the
> last trumpet; for the trumpet will
> sound, and the dead will be raised
> imperishable, and *we will be
> changed*.[204]

Rosh HaShanah is the beginning of the change. What change? It is an agricultural and spiritual change of the year. The crops are gathered in, like the Body of Messiah at the Feast of Trumpets, yet they are transformed to new life in resurrection. Is there a Torah Seed to confirm this, or was Paul mistaken?

 Torah Seed:

> You shall celebrate the Feast of
> Weeks, that is, the first fruits of the
> wheat harvest, and *the Feast of
> Ingathering at the turn of the year.*[205]
> Also you shall observe the Feast of
> the Harvest of the first fruits of your
> labors from what you sow in the field;
> also the Feast of the Ingathering *at*

203. The Babylonian new year *Akitu* fell on the 1st day of Tishrei, which coincided with Yom Teruah on the 1st day of the Seventh Month. When Jews in captivity started calling the Seventh Month by the Babylonian name Tishrei, the rabbis did not want it confused with the pagan new year, so they added the name Rosh Hashanah to Yom Teruah, which eventually became the more common name for this holiday. Shanah's root means a change or transformation, *shinui*. (Ganor, 2016) The transformational theme of Yom Teruah distinguished the Jewish change of the year from Akitu.

204. 1 Co 15:51–52

205. Ex 34:22. The word translated "turn" is *tekufah*: turn or circuit

the end of the year when you gather in the fruit of your labors from the field.[206]

Then Moses commanded them, saying, "At *the end* of every seven years, at the time of the year of remission of debts, at the Feast of Booths...[207]

You are also to count off seven sabbaths of *years* for yourself, seven times seven *years*, so that you have the time of the seven sabbaths of *years*, namely, forty-nine *years*. You shall then sound a ram's horn abroad on the tenth day of the *seventh month*; on the day of atonement you shall sound a horn all through your land.[208]

206. Ex 23:16 The word translated as "end" is *yatza*, the going out, exit

207. Dt 31:10 The word translated as "end" is *ketz*, end

208. Le 25:8-9 This blowing of the ram's horn declares the year of Jubilee when all landholders in Israel return to their land

209. Ex 12:2

210. For an excellent overview of the new moon relative to feast observance and the beginning of the new month and spiritual renewal, see Kisha Gallagher's *The Biblical New Moon: A Beginner's Guide for Celebrating.*

While the first month of the year occurs in the spring, the month of Passover[209] the fall feasts of Trumpets, the Day of Atonement, and Tabernacles mark the end *and* the beginning of a year...in the seventh month. To the Western mind that is conditioned to demand either/or, true or false, this is mind-blowing!

It is no different, however, than looking into the sky over a twenty-four-hour period and seeing two luminaries: the sun by day, and the moon by night. Each serves a similar, but separate function in keeping the Earth in livable balance, but they are not in conflict with the purpose of the other.[210] The sun determines the years, but the moon determines a month. Seeing a Passover slain lamb seated on the Rosh HaShanah living King's throne is not a conflict. A new year of freedom in the Fall does not conflict with the beginning of months in the Spring, and thankfully, both seasons offer prophecies of resurrection in Messiah Yeshua. In fact, the themes of the feasts overlap one another, so they are different, yet they are one, just as the menorah is one piece of beaten gold.

Jewish Tradition: The Sardinians were warned that judgment day would come upon them like a thief if they did not awake. In Jewish tradition, judgment day is Yom Kippur, the Day of Atonement, yet it begins ten days earlier at Rosh HaShanah to awake the "dead" sleeper with a trumpet in time to prepare his garments for resurrection to life instead of leaving them stained for harsh judgment. With Yeshua's advocacy for us with the Father, there is no reason to be caught sleeping, dead in trespass and sin, nor should anyone awaken with stained garments.

There is a Jewish idiom for that awakening day, Rosh HaShanah: "The day and the hour that no man knows..." It may be an allusion to the movement of the cloud in the Torah Seeds of Exodus. Even Moses didn't appear to know, for he also had to wait for the cloud. "And whenever the cloud was lifted from atop the Tent, afterwards the Children of Israel would embark...Sometimes the cloud...for a number of days...sometimes remain...or for a day and a night... or for two days, or a month or a year..." (selected from among 9:15-23).

Torah Seeds: The Sardinians are cautioned how to prepare for a time of tribulation on earth such as has never been seen before. The work of the beast and the dragon will grow intense, and they will make war against the Woman's children who keep the commandments of God and the testimony of Yeshua. To prepare for such an enemy, Exodus 10:9 commands: "When you go to war in your land against the adversary who attacks you, then you shall sound an alarm (*teruah*-shout) with the trumpets, that you may be remembered before the LORD your God, and be saved from your enemies." The shout of the *teruah* calls Adonai to remember them and scatter their enemies.

Jewish tradition: Rosh HaShanah is celebrated as the "day and hour that no man knows" and the "day of the awakening blast," and it is celebrated for two days as a precaution because of the lack of certainty in sighting the new moon marking the date. The *teruah* (shout), *tekiah* (clap), and *shvareem* (wail), are the shofar or horn blasts marking the synagogue services, which are marked by prayers of repentance.

The *tekia* blast of Rosh HaShanah crowns Adonai as King. The long, straight shofar blast is the sound of the King's coronation. *Shvareem* is three wailing, medium blasts resembling the keening/ululation commonly heard in the Middle East both as a celebration sound and a wailing, mourning sound. It demonstrates grief for the shortcomings of the previous year and Israel's recognition of the need for repentance. The *teruah*, which is nine quick blasts, is an alarm clock, arousing Israel from spiritual slumber to seek clarity, alertness, and focus.

The Talmud of Jewish oral law says when there's judgment from below, there's no need for judgment from above. If Jews examine themselves for how they've fallen short in the past and what they expect to change in the future, then there is no need to "wake up" to what is already perceived and sacrificed on the altar of repentance.

211. For an excellent overview of the new moon relative to feast observance and the beginning of the new month and spiritual renewal, see Kisha Gallagher's *The Biblical New Moon: A Beginner's Guide for Celebrating.*

But you have a few people in Sardis who have not soiled their garments; and they will walk with Me in white, for they are worthy.[211]

Torah Seeds: The "few" people in Sardis are representative of the Levites (8:5; 14-19) chosen as redemption in place of the firstborn of the "legions" of the tribes, all listed with their banners and leaders in Chapter Ten. Because they stood with Moses against the worshippers of the

Golden Calf, they were worthy of the priesthood (Exodus 32:25-29). The white garments of the dedicated priesthood are in 8:21 and Exodus 28.

 Jewish tradition: White garments are traditionally worn in the synagogue on the first day of Rosh HaShanah.

> He who overcomes will thus be
> *clothed in white garments;* and I will
> not *erase his name from the book
> of life,* and I will confess his name
> before My Father and before His
> angels.[212]

Torah Seeds: In 8:7, Adonai commands that the Levites wash their garments, "and they shall become pure." In Exodus 8:6, Moses literally clothes Aaron in the priestly garments. The white garments were to be worn in the Holy of Holies beyond the veil rather than the High Priest's colorful, royal attire.

In Exodus 32:32, Moses begs Adonai not to take His Presence from Israel, for he would rather have his own name blotted out of the Book along with his brothers and sisters, even in their failures.

Jewish tradition: New garments are worn at Rosh HaShanah. White is the tradition on first day, and then any color but red on the second day. In some Middle Eastern communities, such as the Baghdadi, white clothes and shoes were also worn at Shavuot, not just Rosh HaShanah and Yom Kippur.[213]

The Rosh HaShanah/Yom Kippur tradition of judgment from the Books is detailed in the Jewish oral law, Mishnah Rosh Hashana 16b, and echoed, in different words, by the Jewish sage Rambam, Hilchos T'shuvah 3:3.

212. Re 3:5

213. Yerushalmi, 2007, Loc. 1754 of 3932

He who has an ear, *let him hear* what the Spirit says to the churches.[214]

 Torah Seed: In Chapter Ten, Moses is commanded to craft two silver trumpets to summon the assembly and signal when the camps were to move. To ignore the trumpets would result in being left behind. Behind left behind should not happen to anyone who keeps the Feast of Trumpets at its appointed time! The teruah blast was to move the Camp to action: "But when you blow an alarm, the camps that are pitched on the east side shall set out..." In Hebrew, the *teruah* also can mean a shout.

Jewish tradition: Hearing the sound of the shofar is the primary commandment of Rosh HaShanah.

Paul in 1 Thessalonians 4: 13-18 uses traditional Jewish themes of Rosh HaShanah to illustrate the return of Yeshua from the shadow seeds of Torah:

> But we do not want you to be uninformed, brethren, about those who are asleep, so that you will not grieve as do the rest who have no hope. For if we believe that Jesus died and rose again, even so God will bring with Him those who have fallen asleep in Jesus. For this we say to you *by the word of the Lord, that we who are alive and remain until the coming of the Lord, will not precede those who have fallen asleep.*

Torah Seed: In the Chapter Twelve finale of *Behaalotkha* is the infamous incident of Aaron and Miriam speaking out about the Cushite woman. In some Jewish literature, it is posited that Miriam was not speaking against the Cushite, but against Moses for withdrawing from conjugal relations with his wife due to his responsibilities. When the cloud departed, Miriam was put outside the Camp with leprosy, which Aaron equates with her being born dead. Figuratively, Miriam is dead outside the Camp and the Presence has withdrawn, causing Aaron and Moses to cry out on her behalf. Neither the cloud nor the Camp moves until she is restored after seven figurative days of death.

Jewish tradition: Death is viewed as "sleep" in Rosh HaShanah literature. Paul writes to the Thessalonians that those who are asleep in Messiah are not without hope, possibly pointing to the strong intercession of Moses and Aaron on behalf of Miriam. Both Moses the lawgiver and Aaron the Light-bringer pray for restoration so that the *entire* Camp may once again move. Miriam's resurrection from the dead preceded the gathering of "living" Israel into the clouds for forward movement.

> For *the Lord Himself will descend from heaven with a shout, with the voice of the archangel and with the trumpet of God*, and the dead in Christ will rise first.[215]

> God has *ascended* with a *shout*, the LORD, *with the sound of a trumpet*.[216]

Torah Seeds: It was the Lord Himself, the Angel of the Presence, who descended in the cloud to speak with Moses; the Name was in Him to heal and to forgive sins. When Aaron and Miriam spoke against the Cushite, "The LORD descended in a pillar of cloud and stood at the entrance to the Tent of Meeting..." (12:5).

> But when you blow an alarm (*teruah-shout*), the camps that are pitched on the east side shall set out.

Jewish tradition: The pillar descended, but when it was time to ascend, a shout signaled that the people were to move with His Presence. Jewish tradition affirms the rest of Paul's exhortation to the Thessalonians: "Then we who are alive and remain will be caught up together with them in the clouds to meet the Lord in the air, and so we shall always be with the Lord."

Torah seed:

And whenever the cloud was lifted
from atop the Tent, afterwards the
Children of Israel would embark,
and in the place where the cloud
would rest, there the Children of
Israel would encamp. Sometimes
the cloud...for a number of days...
sometimes remain...or for a day and
a night...or for two days, or a month
or a year... (selected from among
Exodus 9:15-23).

The cloud was over them by day
when they journeyed from the
camp. When the Ark would travel,
Moses would say, 'Arise, HaShem,
and let Your foes be scattered,
let those who hate You flee from
before You.' And when it rested, he
would say, 'Return, HaShem, to the
myriad thousands of Israel" (10:34-35
Artscroll TANAKH).

The return of "the Lord Himself" in the letter to the Thessalonians parallels the movement of the cloud/ ark in the wilderness. The movement of the cloud was matched by the movement of the Ark carrying the Word of God.

Jewish tradition: The cloud/Word scattered the enemy, and then it returned to the myriad thousands of Israel, which matches Paul's description of the gathering of the saints. The cloud of the Angel of the Presence was centered at the "Tent of Meeting,"[217] suggesting it as the standard and rallying point for all Israel in the resurrection.

The Greek word *aer* translated "in the air" in 1 Thessalonians Four refers to breathable air close to the earth. It does not imply clouds high above the earth. This is congruent with the Jewish tradition that the Israelites walked in "clouds of glory" in the wilderness, for from the many passages about the movement of the cloud in the wilderness and the initial camp at Sukkot, they derive that Israel entered into Sukkot (Tabernacle) clouds of glory when they exited Egypt.

> Who was at the forefront of the Camp's movement? Judah. After the Babylonian exile, any of the tribes who still had their tribal identity called themselves "Jews." Could this arrangement be a Torah shadow-Seed from which the plant and fruit of Jewish leadership in the Shabbat, the moedim, and Temple services grows?

> Behold, on the mountains the feet of him who brings good news, who announces peace! Celebrate your feasts, *O Judah*; pay your vows. For never again will the wicked one pass through you; he is cut off completely.[218]

> Then the word of the LORD of hosts came to me, saying, 'Thus says the LORD of hosts, "'The fast of the

217. The Tabernacle was also called *the Ohel Moed*, or Tent of Appointed Time, a reference to the moedim, the feasts of Adonai during which all Israel gathered to worship.

218. Nah 1:15

fourth, the fast of the fifth, the fast of the seventh and the fast of the tenth months will become joy, gladness, and cheerful feasts for the *house of Judah*; so love truth and peace...
It will yet be that peoples will come, even the inhabitants of many cities. The inhabitants of one will go to another, saying, """Let us go at once to entreat the favor of the LORD, and to seek the LORD of hosts; I will also go.'""" So many peoples and mighty nations will come to seek the LORD of hosts in Jerusalem and to entreat the favor of the LORD...
In those days ten men from all the nations will grasp *the garment of a Jew*, saying, 'Let us go with you, for we have heard that God is with you.'[219]

Then what advantage has *the Jew*? Or what is the benefit of circumcision? Great in every respect. First of all, that they were entrusted with the oracles of God.[220]

...who are Israelites, to whom belongs the adoption as sons, and the glory and the covenants and the giving of the Law and the temple service and the promises...[221]

219. Zec 8:19-23

220. Ro 3:1-2

221. Ro 9:4-5

222. Even the Assembly at Laodicea in Revelation holds Jewish tradition, which assigns the scales of justice as a theme of the month of Tishrei, the Seventh Month. Laodicea means "justice of the peoples."

223. The Jewish sages do not attempt to rationalize all of the rabbinic laws, for the "motivation in enacting laws was to protect the laws of the Torah. As a general rule, Chazal (the sages) did not make laws to protect other rabbinic laws...

Judah is at the forefront of the Camp's movement, and according to Nahum, Zechariah, and Paul, they also are charged with the primary responsibility of safeguarding both the prescribed weighty moedim as well as any "lighter" additional fasts or feasts of tradition. Zechariah does not object to Judah's addition of fast days to Yom Kippur, rather, by describing how they will be transformed to joy for all nations[222] in Messiah's reign, Zechariah validates

140

as helpful what some may judge an addition to the Torah. What Judah grew from the seed of the Torah was a good tradition that foreshadowed Israel's resurrection life in Messiah.

It would be a grave mistake to elevate Jewish traditions above the Torah, which casts the perfect shadow; however, to completely disregard Jewish tradition would be to lose the context of much of Scripture, especially the Newer Testament, which teaches a transformed heart, not a transformed Torah. Without any frame of instructional reference for observance, practice in a Torah walk can become increasingly bizarre as the learner remains blind to the movement of the Camp led by Judah... who was led of the Angel of the Presence. This is both a Seed and shadow of the reality in the Lion of Judah. The result of total disregard for Judah's scepter is family division, unceasing arguments, and wayward disunity.

While there may be some unfathomable traditions, fables, or customs within Judaism,[223] exercise caution in the daily walk. The body of Jewish oral law has increased exponentially since the First Century believers were educated in some of the customs, so gathering a body of believers is a challenge when so many despair of finding the "right," "correct," or "truthful" methods of observance.

This is a transition generation just like the First Century, a generation in which it is possible to put faith in Yeshua as the Messiah as well as to faithfully observe the Father's commandments. Abiding in the cloud and with the crowd can be a challenge, especially when at the extremes some have fallen in love with anything Jewish, while others abhor anything "rabbinic." Take His Hand, Yeshua, the authority. Keep an eye on Judah for movement and rest times in order to stay in and under the cloud. The Levites gather,[224] and Judah is the royalty of covering authority. Avoid tare-ditions, but don't label as sin

(223, continued) it does not mean that gezerot do not have an internal logic and mechanism. Therefore, while the ultimate motivation for the gezerah is to protect a Torah law, the result of the gezerah may affect actions that would be seemingly disconnected from protecting Torah law." (Appel, 2016, p. 97)

224. Levi's birth order is a hint. His birth order of third corresponds to the Third Day when the waters were gathered, signifying his Levitical role in gathering Israel to the Tent of Meeting. Immersion and sprinkling with water is a vital part of the Levitical rituals in the books of Leviticus and Numbers. The firstborn Reuben is described as "unstable as water," like the chaos of the deep on Day One.

Jewish traditions grown from the Seed *and* good soil.

> At the command of the LORD
> they remained encamped, and at
> the command of the LORD they
> journeyed; they kept the charge of
> the LORD, at the command of the
> LORD   by the hand of Moses.[225]

> So they departed from the mountain
> of the LORD on a journey of three
> days; and the ark of the covenant
> of the LORD went before them for
> the *three days' journey*, to *search
> out a resting place for them*. And the
> cloud of the LORD was above them
> by day when they went out from the
> camp.[226]

It is a three-day journey to rest, and the three days were a symbol to which Yeshua repeatedly alluded. The gathering at the Passover season on the third feast, Firstfruits, is a first resurrection. Will we walk in the clouds from the Day of the Awakening Blast to Sukkot? Yeshua is the Angel of the Presence in the cloud, and he is covering, clothing, speaking to, and resurrecting Israel. That same Hand is judging those on the earth who are weighed in the balances and found wanting. Clouds make a shadow in the earth on a sunny day, but the sun does not make clear shadows in the day of darkness. Instead, the reality is found in Messiah, who is in the cloud with his witnesses.

225. Nu 9: 23

226. Nu 10:33-34

SECTION II

WHAT
HAPPENS?

11

BEWARE THE WIZARD

Section I of this booklet examined Scriptures as well as traditional Jewish sources. In Section II, further investigation into life after death also correlates Scriptures with traditional Jewish sources. A word of caution is in order. The Word has harsh things to say about a *baal ob*, a person who has a "familiar spirit," and a *yidd'oni*, a "wizard." Both are to be stoned if they practice contacting the dead or raising up the souls of the dead to communicate with them. Any investigation of the dead should take a wide path around anything that teaches or practices necromancy or magic.

Understanding resurrection must be anchored in Biblical patterns, and when outside sources are examined, they must be proofed against the Biblical text. Peer review of one's conclusions is important so that one doesn't become "carried away." Very few people have died, resurrected, and written books about it, so we have little to rely upon for factual information. Even the risen Yeshua's recorded statements are few relative to our many questions.

For that reason, the author requests that the reader approach this section with due caution. Correlations to Biblical and rabbinic texts are offered for consideration, but beware and guard the heart against excessive fascination with death, angels, or demons. Such obsession can be a symptom of covetousness, which gives a foothold to dark forces.

There is evil in the world, whether it is seen or unseen. The wizard or necromancer (also called a medium) either deceives his paying victim into believing that he has accessed the dead or he actually taps into the realm of the dead. Curiosity or inappropriate attachment to a dead loved one can cause one to put one's self under the influence of a forbidden relationship with a wizard and the realm of the dead and demonic activity.

Always, always, satisfy curiosity about the dead with the Holy Scriptures. The hidden things belong to God, but Scripture reveals what He wants us to know with certainty. Section II is more of a discussion of how the Scriptures and Jewish tradition point to certain principles of the resurrection rather than a doctrine. The principles are presented for your consideration and hopefully, for comfort.

12

LIKE ANGELS

What will resurrection be like? Yeshua taught many times about the resurrection, which, to the Pharisees, was old news. To the Sadducees, however, Yeshua taught some of the most specific information about the resurrection, and the Sadducees didn't even believe in the resurrection. Because of this, they often challenged Yeshua to trap him, and unwittingly, they drew out of him the teaching of resurrection that gives the details we want!

> For in the resurrection they neither marry nor are given in marriage, but are *like angels* in heaven.[227]

> For when they rise from the dead, they neither marry nor are given in marriage, but are *like angels* in heaven.[228]

> Jesus said to them, "The sons of this age marry and are given in marriage, but those who are considered worthy to attain to that age and the resurrection from the dead, neither marry nor are given in marriage; for they cannot even

227. Mt 22:30

228. Mk 12:25

die anymore, because they are *like angels*, and are sons of God, being sons of the resurrection. But that the dead are raised, even Moses showed, *in the passage about the burning bush*, where he calls the Lord THE GOD OF ABRAHAM, AND THE GOD OF ISAAC, AND THE GOD OF JACOB....[229]

All three Gospel accounts of this conversation between the Sadducees, who did not believe in the resurrection, and Yeshua, who IS the resurrection, are linked to the burning bush. Life expectancy is not usually long for those who hear a voice out of fire: "Has *any* people heard the voice of God speaking from the midst of the fire, as you have heard *it*, and survived?"[230] Moses survived the burning bush, and the Israelites survived the fire on Mount Sinai. Jewish tradition is that at each Divine utterance of the Ten Commandments, the Israelites died and were resurrected, until after Ten, they begged Moses to go hear the rest and pass it on to them:

> You said, 'Behold, the Lord our God has shown us His glory and His greatness, and we have heard His voice from the midst of the fire; we have seen today that God speaks with man, yet he lives. Now then why should we die? For this great fire will consume us; if we hear the voice of the Lord our God any longer, then we will die.'[231]

More than Ten was just too much resurrection! Yeshua came to give Israel life in the commandments through the Holy Spirit so that once and for all Israel can resurrect to life in them.

Yeshua reminds the Sadducees that God is the God of "Abraham, Isaac, and Jacob," which means that

229. Lk 20:34-37

230. Dt 4:33

231. Dt 5:24-35

these three men still live beyond the grave. They can (and would be) resurrected with Yeshua:

> The tombs were opened, and many bodies of the saints who had fallen asleep were raised; and coming out of the tombs after His resurrection they entered the holy city and appeared to many.[232]

Since the question is one of resurrection, and Yeshua so consistently relates it to Abraham, Isaac, and Jacob, the reader must visit the significance of the burial place of the patriarchs and matriarchs, the town of Hebron. They were buried with their wives, Sarah, Rebekah, and Leah, in the Cave of Machpelah. The Jewish sages explain that the site was important as a burial place to Abraham because Adam and Eve were buried there. Imagine Eve, who was first called "Ishah," or wife, weeping as they exited the Garden. In the mystical tradition of Judaism, the Cave of Machpelah is a spiritual gateway to the Garden of Eden.[233] It is a passageway or tunnel that bridges life and death.

Isaac and Rebekah's are the only tomb pair in the Cave of Machpelah today who are withheld from the general public. It is guarded by the Waqf so that Jews and Christians may not approach. If Isaac is the paleo-prophecy of resurrection, and he was an olah offering that pictures how the Bride of Messiah ascends as a "fire" or "wife" in the flames, there is true irony.

The Gospel of John is the only one that does not record that "like angels" resurrection conversation between the Sadducees and Yeshua, but did John leave a connecting clue? In his record of the resurrection, John narrates a puzzling and mystical account that is packed with important details. Read the following passage carefully, focusing on the dialogue between Yeshua and Miriam (Mary):

232. Mt 27:52-53

233. Raphael, p. 380

But Mary stood outside **by the tomb** weeping, and as she wept she stooped down and looked into the tomb. And she saw two angels in white sitting, one at the head and the other at the feet, where the body of Jesus had lain. Then they said to her, 'Woman, why are you weeping?'

She said to them, 'Because they have taken away my Lord, and I do not know where they have laid Him.'

Now when she had said this, **she turned around** and saw Jesus standing there, and did not know that it was Jesus. Jesus said to her, 'Woman, why are you weeping? Whom are you seeking?'

She, supposing Him to be **the gardener**, said to Him, Sir, if You have carried Him away, tell me where You have laid Him, and I will take Him away.

Jesus said to her, 'Mary [Miriam]!'

She turned and said to Him, **'Rabboni!' (which is to say, Teacher).**

Jesus said to her, 'Do not cling to Me, for I have not yet **ascended** to My Father; but go to My brethren and say to them, "'**I am ascending to My Father** and your Father, and to My God and your God.'"

Mary Magdalene came and told the disciples that she had seen the Lord, and that He had spoken these things to her.[234]

In summary, Miriam speaks with two angels. She turns around and sees "Jesus," whom she supposes is the gardener, for she is now looking into the garden, not the tomb. She speaks to this gardener Yeshua, but then, Jesus says, "Miriam," and Miriam turns *again* to speak to him. This is not a mistranslation of the

234. Jn 20:11-18 NKJV

150

Greek text, for the King James version is preserving the oddity of this exchange. Mary turns *twice* to address Yeshua.

Who might the first "gardener Yeshua" symbolize? Jewish literature asserts:

> ...when a man departs from the world...[he] meets Adam the first man, sitting at the gate of Gan Eden...ready to welcome with joy all those who have observed the commands of their Master.[235]

The reader has several word clues: angels, tomb, gardener, ascend, Father, God. The setting? A garden and a burial tomb. Apply the Rule of First Mention to find the beginning of the thread. The first gardener and garden? The first man, Adam, and the Garden of Eden. The first burial tomb? The Cave of Machpelah. The first angels? The two angels guarding the entrance to the Garden of Eden. This time, however, the two angels are not holding a sword that guards the way to the Tree of Life. Miriam is observing a step in the process of resurrection (ascending), and she sees the way back to the Tree of Life in her Teacher Yeshua, the Living Word.

Are these two tomb angels only representative of the two cherubim guarding the Garden, though? Scripture records different classes or hierarchies of angels. One type of angel very much resembles human beings, and human beings are often unaware that they are angels until they choose to reveal themselves. Some angels are fierce warriors, such as Michael, Gabriel, the angel who confronted Joshua, or the ones that were at Yeshua's disposal:

> Or do you think that I cannot appeal to My Father, and He will at once put at My disposal more than twelve legions of angels?[236]

235. Raphael, p. 309

236. Mt 25:53

An encounter with these warrior angels is both memorable and frightening.

The "man-like" angels, however, can eat and drink like the angels who visited Abraham, and even wrestle, like the "man" angel who wrestled with Jacob. This class of angels is called *Ishim* by the rabbis, for the angel that wrestled with Jacob is called an *ish* (man) in Genesis 32:24. Ishim would be the plural of *ish*, but there is a grammatical difference between men (*anashim*) and angels (*ishim*).

This grammatical designation helps the reader to differentiate between mortal men and angels with a man-like appearance. One thing to remember about ishim, however, is that they, too, can have a very fierce appearance. The angel who confronted Joshua in 5:13 is called an *ish*.

Now Yeshua's resurrection statement has context. We will be like angels. Which angels? Most likely, the ishim who retain a man-like appearance, yet they have supernatural strength, intelligence, and many other attributes that comic-book and superhero script-writers put into their stories. Even before his resurrection, however, Messiah Yeshua had supernatural, miraculous qualities. The resurrected Yeshua ate fish, cooked, walked with his own disciples on the road to Emmaus unrecognized, and he had a body. His characteristics were very much like the ishim class of angels.

Why the ishim class? Perhaps the risen Yeshua can manifest himself as anything the Father wants, yet it is primarily the ishim who bring messages from Heaven to mankind. Yeshua taught that our resurrection will transform the resurrected righteous to ishim-like forms, and the Father presented the Son to mankind thus. The two angels guarding the tomb have the appearance of ishim, and they wear white, just as the righteous, resurrected dead are clothed.

Angel-worship is dangerous, and some people carry little angel images as good-luck charms or decorations. The ishim and other classes of angels neither desire, nor can they accept, such attention.[237] The ishim are created beings like the *anashim* (human beings), and their forms should only be reproduced by Heavenly edict, such as the commanded Tabernacle weavings and cherubim guarding the Ark.

Yeshua, however, offers his students the example of the ishim to help them visualize their post-resurrection bodies, and Miriam sees two examples of angels in the tomb of the garden and two examples of Yeshua in the garden. In Mark, one of the two angels described in John is a "young man," and in Luke, "two men":

> Entering the tomb, they saw *a young man* sitting at the right, wearing a white robe; and they were amazed.[238]

> While they were perplexed about this, behold, two men suddenly stood near them in dazzling clothing;[239]

Resurrection bodies are described with a few important characteristics of ishim:

- purity of garments
- brightness
- message-bearers (servants) of Heaven

One thing to remember, however, is that Yeshua taught that the resurrected dead would be *like* angels. Mankind is a separate creation, and it would be a mistake to reduce our expectation to simply becoming another class of created being. Just as man is made *in the image* of Elohim, yet he is not Elohim, so humans can *be like* ishim, yet not ishim.

237. Re 19:10; 22:9

238. Mk 16:6

239. Lk 24:4

13

GATEWAY TO THE GARDEN

When Abraham was asked to offer Isaac as an *olah* offering, there is no record of his words, only his obedience. In synagogues at Rosh HaShanah, the service is accompanied by the reading of the Akeidah, the passage of Scripture describing the binding of Isaac as an *olah* sacrifice. An olah is usually translated "whole burnt offering," but in Hebrew, it means to go up, as in the resurrection. A Jew who moves from any other country to Israel "makes Aliyah," or goes up to his covenant homeland. The natural Land of Israel represents the spiritual realm hovering just above it.

In the prayers of Rosh HaShanah, forgiveness is not requested as it is ten days later at Yom Kippur. Instead, the entreaty for forgiveness is made with the sound of the shofar,[240] a song of intense spiritual power offered through the horn of an animal. The voice of the shofar freely moved between the physical and spiritual realms at Sinai, for the people "saw" the sounds![241]

While the binding of Isaac focuses on the practical actions of Abraham in sacrificing his son, and Scripture uses the sacrifice as a prophecy of resurrection, the text has given Jewish scholars something to ponder

240. A shofar is a trumpet made from the horn of an animal, such as a ram or ibex. In tradition, the ram caught in the thicket who was substituted for Isaac supplied two shofars: the Last Trump at Rosh HaShanah (resurrection of the dead), and the Great Trump at Yom Kippur ten days later.

241. "Then the LORD spoke to you from the midst of the fire; you heard the sound of words, but you saw no form—only a voice." (Dt 4:12)

in Sarah's absence. Sarah is not in Be'er Sheva when Abraham returns, but Hebron. Genesis 23:2 cites "Kiryat Arba," which is in Hebron. Consider Hebron the larger area, and Kiryat Arba the specific area within the larger, such as the city of Lexington in Fayette County.

The overlay of Hebron onto Kiryat Arba has linguistic significance. Kiryat Arba means "City of Four." Another city is described in Revelation as built four-square:

> The city is laid out as a *square*; its length is as great as its breadth. And he measured the city with the reed: twelve thousand furlongs. Its length, breadth, and height are equal.[242]

> The city had no need of the sun or of the moon to shine in it, for the glory of God illuminated it. The Lamb is its light. *And the nations* of those who are saved shall walk in its light, and *the kings of the earth* bring their glory and honor into it. Its gates shall not be shut at all by day (there shall be no night there). And they shall bring the glory and the honor of the nations into it.[243]

The location of Sarah's burial cave, Machpelah, in Kiryat Arba, City of Four, connects the reader to the New Jerusalem, a place where the nations will bring glory and honor. Sarah is the woman prophesied to be the mother of many nations, and that kings of peoples would descend from her:

242. Re 21:16

243. Re 21:23-26

244. Ge 17:16
KJV

> And I will bless her, and give thee a son also of her: yea, I will bless her, and she shall be a *mother of nations*; *kings of people* shall be of her.[244]

The Cave of Machpelah is known as the Cave of the Couples or the Cave of Doubles. The patriarchs and matriarchs are buried in pairs. According to rabbinic tradition, the reason that Sarah was at Hebron was to intercede on behalf of Isaac. Abraham saddled a donkey, set out with his "young men," and went to Mount Moriah, the current-day Temple Mount, to sacrifice Isaac.

Abraham believed that God would even resurrect Isaac from the dead, but Sarah goes to the tomb of Adam and Eve to intercede for Isaac:

> That is what the Scriptures mean when God told him, 'I have made you the father of many nations.' This happened *because Abraham believed in the God who brings the dead back to life* and who creates new things out of nothing.[245]

> By faith Abraham, when he was tested, offered up Isaac, and he who had received the promises was offering up his only begotten son; it was he to whom it was said, "IN ISAAC YOUR DESCENDANTS SHALL BE CALLED." *He considered that God is able to raise people even from the dead, from which he also received him back as a type.*[246]

> And so it happened just as the Scriptures say: 'Abraham believed God, and God counted him as righteous because of his faith.' He was even called *the friend of God*.[247]

According to the tradition, Sarah grieves and weeps herself to death, and this is why Abraham doesn't return to Be'er Sheva (Beer Sheba), but instead goes to Hebron to bury Sarah. Hebron was the place of

245. Ro 4:17

246. He 11:17-19

247. Ja 2:23

the "Covenant between the Pieces" and where God had sent messengers to tell the couple that they would miraculously have a son. According to the tradition, Sarah prayed until her heart gave out. "Abraham came there to bury, eulogize and weep over his beloved wife, without whom he understood that his life with God was over, but through whom the destiny of Israel had been secured forever."[248] Although Abraham's life with God was not literally over, his spiritual significance fades from the text and is transferred to the next generation, Isaac.

The root of the word Hebron is *chavar*, which is also the Hebrew root of "friend." Because of Abraham's faith, he was called a friend of God. What merited Sarah to be buried in the tomb beside Adam and Eve in Hebron?

To Eve was given the prophecy of the Seed of the Woman: the Messiah would be the Seed of the Woman who would crush the head of the serpent. After sin entered the world, Adam names Eve in Hebrew "Chavah," or "The Mother of All Living." Before that, she was *Ishah*. Ishah means both woman and wife.

> And Adam said, 'This is now bone
> of my bones, and flesh of my flesh:
> she shall be called Woman [*Ishah*],
> because she was taken out of
> Man.'[249]

In the Garden account of Yeshua, the Gardener, and the Angels at the tomb, both the angels and Yeshua "the gardener" address Miriam by calling her "Woman," before Yeshua calls her by her name Miriam. They all ask, "Woman, why are you weeping?" The Hebrew word for woman is *ishah*. The angels and Yeshua address Miriam with the same name as pre-sin Eve:[250]

> And they said to her, '*Woman, why*

248. Riskin, 2015

249. Ge 2:23

250. Jn 20:13, 15

are you weeping?' She said to them,
'Because they have taken away my
Lord, and I do not know where they
have laid Him.'

Jesus said to her, '*Woman, why
are you weeping?* Whom are you
seeking?' Supposing Him to be *the
gardener*, she said to Him, 'Sir, if
you have carried Him away, tell me
where you have laid Him, and I will
take Him away.'[251]

When "the gardener," which recalls the First Adam,
addresses Miriam as Ishah, she turns to him, but when
Yeshua uses Miriam's actual name, she turns again
to speak to Yeshua. One has to wonder from what
realm Miriam turns from the address Ishah, the first
name of Eve, to speak to the other one who calls her
"Miriam."

In the Book of Revelation, the first seven mentions of
"the woman" are positive, describing the virtuous
woman Israel.[252] The next five mentions are negative,
referring to the adulterous woman who rides the
scarlet beast.[253] To match these twelve mentions
of the woman and adulterous wife in two chapters
of Revelation, Genesis Chapters Two and Three
mention ishah twelve times as her name Woman
or wife before the curse of sin enters the marriage.
After that, Adam names his wife Chavah (Eve).

When Adam and Eve are sought in the Garden
by Elohim after their sin, He uses the question,
"Eikha?" *Where are you?* If pronounced slightly
differently, the same Hebrew word *eikha* also means
lamentation and mourning, such as the Hebrew title
of the book of Lamentations. In the Garden, it hints
that even Elohim can experience mourning at His
creation's loss of their place in the Lower Garden.
They have spiritually descended, making it harder
for them to "see" Him in their daily walk with Him.

251. Jn 20:15

252. Re 12:4, 6,
13, 14, 15, 16,
& 17, and "a
woman" in Re
12:1

253. Re 17:4, 6,
7, 9, 18, and "a
woman" in Re
17:3

Likewise, in Lamentations, the Prophet Jeremiah laments Israel's loss of spiritual and natural home, the Temple, Jerusalem, and the Land of Israel itself. Both are expressions of mourning for loss of place and relationship with the Father.

Sarah, like Abram, has a blessing in her name change from Sarai to Sarah. She becomes the Mother of Many Nations who will be blessed from Abraham and Sarah. In Revelation, her children, the Children of Israel, keep the testimony of Yeshua and the commandments of God. They have a love relationship to the commandments.

Paul tries to explain in Galatians 4:22-31 about mankind's Mother Sarah, who is Jerusalem above, the wife of Abraham's heart. Her blessing will prevail in the righteous. Those who are the seed of the Harlot, those who ride the scarlet beast, will be cursed. They are descended from Hagar below, whose relationship with Abraham was one of slavery. Those who have a slavish relationship to the commandments are not born of the Spirit above.

Abraham and Sarah's seed was Isaac, who prefigured Messiah Yeshua. While it was Abraham's job to sacrifice him, it was Sarah's to intercede for his resurrection in grief and weeping. This intercessory sacrifice was unto death for her, yet Abraham's sacrifice of Isaac earned him the title of the Friend of God on the Temple Mount:

> Did You not, O our God, drive out
> the inhabitants of this land before
> Your people Israel and give it to the
> descendants of *Abraham Your friend*
> forever?[254]

This title of "friend" is not from the root *chavar*, but *ahav*, beloved. Because Abraham offers his only son "whom you love (*ahav*)," Abraham becomes the beloved friend of God. In the same chapter of

254. 2 Ch 20:7

Hebrews that describes the faith of Abraham in the resurrection, "women" are described as well:

> Women received back their dead
> by resurrection; and others were
> tortured, not accepting their release,
> *so that they might obtain a better
> resurrection;*[255]

In the pages of the TANAKH (Old Testament), only a few women received back their dead by resurrection. Is Sarah one of them? Yes and no. Sarah did not live to see Isaac's resurrection; instead, she died a torturous death of grief and weeping for her only son. Somehow, the writer of Hebrews suggests, her torture brought about a better resurrection. That resurrection could only be the resurrection of Yeshua. Because of her death, Abraham purchases the burial ground of Adam and Eve in Hebron, the legendary gateway back to the Garden.

255. He 11:35

14

INTO THE GARDEN

Sarah's weeping for the resurrection and Eve's sorrow is mirrored by Miriam's weeping in the Garden as she searches for the body of Yeshua. Perhaps Abraham's two "young men" go to the tomb of Machpelah to bring news of Isaac's resurrection. It is as though we can see Sarah weeping for Isaac in Miriam's visit to the Garden tomb. Suddenly, Miriam sees two ishim, and she realizes that there is no corpse in the tomb. She turns to speak to a gardener, but as with ishim, she doesn't at first recognize that he's not a normal human being. Who is he? The first gardener, Adam, whose body has finally been awakened from his place at Machpelah to be restored to his soul by Yeshua? In Miriam, one may see the hope of Mother Sarah, who wept herself to death for a better resurrection at the spiritual gateway to the Garden.

Miriam is in a garden, but what Garden is it? Is it merely a garden adjacent to a burial tomb, or is she experiencing something much more spiritual? Jewish tradition concerning death and resurrection, as well as Scripture, may supply the missing link. That which was the gateway to death has become the gateway to resurrection in Yeshua. It's an up-and-down experience.

Gan Eden, the Garden of Eden, is the Lower Garden, sometimes called Paradise. The Upper Garden is in a higher Heaven. The Lower Garden, or Gan Eden, is a place of teaching and learning in order to ascend to the Father. It was mankind's first domain. Miriam's first reaction to seeing Yeshua is "Rabboni,"[256] or Teacher. Not Master, the term she's used for the ishim and the "first" Yeshua, but Teacher. The Lower Garden of Paradise is the realm of the Kingdom associated with learning in order to ascend to the higher realm.

> O people in Zion, inhabitant in
> Jerusalem, *you will weep no longer*.
> He will surely be gracious to you
> at the sound of your cry; when He
> hears it, He will answer you. Although
> the Lord has given you bread of
> privation and water of oppression,
> *He, your Teacher will no longer hide
> Himself, but your eyes will behold
> your Teacher*.[257]

The Jewish sage Rashi expounds upon Isaiah 30:20, linking it to Numbers 23:23:

> At the proper time it shall be said to
> Jacob and to Israel, what [miracle]
> God has done!

This passage in Numbers is part of the reluctant prophet Balaam's vision of Israel. This miraculous event that will occur in Israel has context in Numbers 23:21:

> He has not observed misfortune in
> Jacob; nor has He seen trouble in
> Israel;
>
> The LORD his God is with him, and
> *the shout* of a king is among them.

256. Mary answers Yeshua in Hebrew in the Garden. Is this our post-mortem, resurrection language? If so, then it's a good thing one comes into the Kingdom as a little child... it's much easier to learn a new language!

257. Is 30:19-20

Balaam prophesies of a time when miraculously, trouble will not be found in Israel because of the "shout" of a king among them and the Holy One Himself is with him. The play-on word of "shout" in Hebrew denotes the sound of a shofar, *teruah*, which is associated with the Feast of Trumpets (Rosh HaShanah) and the First Resurrection.

Because Yeshua was resurrected on the Third Day, the Feast of Firstfruits, his disciples have hope of resurrection on the Fifth Day, the Feast of Trumpets. According to Rashi's commentary to Numbers 23, the miracle that takes place because of the shout of the king is that the dearness that Balaam pronounced over Israel will be revealed to all nations, for Israel will sit before Him and learn Torah from His mouth.

> Their realm will be further in, i.e., closer to God, than the ministering angels, and the angels will ask Israel, 'What has God wrought?' This is the meaning of that which it says, 'And your eyes shall see your Teacher.'[258]

Significantly, in the garden, Yeshua tells Miriam to stop clinging to him because he must ascend to the Father. The Upper Garden was closer to the Presence than the Lower Garden, the preparation and teaching place, which is also a work and resting place. Only the priests were allowed to advance beyond the altar of burnt offerings to the Holy Place,[259] and one might speculate that Miriam could ascend no further with Yeshua...yet.

Somewhere between Jerusalem and the outskirts of Hebron is a spring known as Ein Eitam. An ancient aqueduct carried water from Hebron and Bethlehem to Jerusalem:

> The aqueduct begins at the Ein Eitam spring near Solomon's Pools south of Bethlehem and stretches 21

258. Rashi to Numbers 23:23, p. 298

259. Lieber, p. 621

kilometers to Jerusalem. 'Despite its length, it flows along a very gentle downward slope whereby the water level falls just one meter per kilometer of distance.'[260]

The waters of this spring were located 23 *amot* (cubits) higher than the floor of the Temple. From at least the times of the Hasmoneans, an aqueduct flowed from the Hebron spring into the *mikveh* in which the High Priest immersed himself on Yom Kippur for his service in the Temple:

> Five immersions and ten sanctifications the High Priest immerses and sanctifies his hands and feet, respectively, on the day of Yom Kippur. And all of these immersions and sanctifications take place in the sacred area, the Temple courtyard, in the Hall of Parva... Abaye said: 'Conclude...that Ein Eitam, the spring from which water was supplied to the Temple, was twenty-three cubits higher than the ground of the Temple courtyard.'[261]

260. By TOI STAFF. 21 May 2015. *The Times of Israel.* "Section of Ancient Jerusalem Aqueduct Uncovered." https://www. timesofisrael.com / section- of-ancient- jerusalem- aqueduct- uncovered/

261. Yoma 31a

Although Yeshua's resurrection occurred in the week of Passover, all seven festivals of Israel have interlocking and overlapping themes, giving them unity. Each prescribed feast prophesied something of the Divine plan for salvation, redemption, and return to the Garden. As a type and shadow of Messiah, the High Priest immersed before the Yom Kippur service in the pool of water supplied by the Ein Eitam spring at Hebron. The aqueduct flowed through Bethlehem, the place of Yeshua's birth, and terminated in the Temple courtyard. From there, the High Priest could make atonement for sin each year.

Miriam sees Yeshua in a garden before he ascends to the Father in the Upper Garden of the Throne, so he must rise to another level than that which Miriam sees. Jewish tradition says that the souls of the righteous dead are located under the Throne of Adonai. Perhaps this is a description of the Lower Garden, the place designed for mankind:

> Thus says the LORD, 'Heaven is My throne and the earth is My footstool. Where then is a house you could build for Me? And where is a place that I may rest?'[262]

Before sin, the natural and spiritual realms of earth were one, the Garden of Eden. It would have placed Adam and Eve's Garden realm under the Throne of the Holy One. He would descend from His upper realm in the cool of the evening to fellowship, specifically "walk" in the Garden with them. In that sense, the footstool comparison makes sense, for it is related to the "feet" of the Holy One. Hebrews 1:13 points out prophecy from Psalm 110:1, relating specifically to Yeshua:

> But to which of the angels has He ever said, SIT AT MY RIGHT HAND, UNTIL I MAKE YOUR ENEMIES A FOOTSTOOL FOR YOUR FEET?

The simple sense of the promise is that Yeshua's enemies will be subdued. In a larger sense, though, when Yeshua's body of believers is resurrected from the dead, they will rise to the cloud, leaving the unbeliever, the enemy, or the unprepared behind. The enemy will remain in the fallen realm of earth without enjoying the realm of spiritual and physical unity in Gan Eden. The Garden may be a realm beneath the Throne, yet it is higher than the natural world alone and Sheol (hell). Like angels, those who are resurrected to Gan Eden enjoy the ability to move between natural and supernatural realms of earth, unlike those who are relegated to remain at "foot" level.

262. Is 66:1

So it is "women" who receive their dead back by resurrection,[263] but at Hebron, Sarah prayed and died for a better resurrection even than her own son Isaac. She had faith in the resurrection of a Messiah, Yeshua. From that faith sprang the water that would supply the High Priest of the Temple. His prayers, service, and incense would arise on Yom Kippur from the various symbolic Temple stations that reflected how the atonement for sin was occurring simultaneously in the Upper Chamber of the Throne. Yeshua embodied both salvation from death and the service of forgiveness of sin.

Ein Eitam means "spring of the bird's lair." Although it is unknown how exactly Jewish tradition coined the phrase, the Palace of Messiah in the Lower Garden is called Kan Tzippor, or the Bird's Nest. Perhaps the ancient aqueduct from the bird's lair is a mysterious geographic code connecting the resurrection faith of Hebron to the birthplace of Messiah Yeshua in Bethlehem to Messiah's Palace on the Temple Mount.

> Ein Eitam in Hebron flows to
> ▼
> Bethlehem and then to
> ▼
> The Temple in Jerusalem

---

263. He 11:35

15

RESPECT FOR THE DEAD

The death of Nadab and Avihu in Leviticus 10 yielded important instructions for death, burial, and mourning. In spite of the death of both sons and brothers, Aaron, Itamar, and Eleazer were not permitted to leave the Mishkan[264] because the anointing oil was still upon them. They were not permitted to 1) let their hair go unkempt 2) tear their clothes or 3) wail, weep.

These are established rituals of mourning for the seven classes of people one is obliged to mourn: father, mother, brother, sister, son, daughter, spouse. We can mourn for more than those seven required relationships, but one is required to mourn for those seven. The whole congregation of Israel mourned for Moses and Aaron. You can add more, but not decrease.

In modern Judaism, those rituals are observed during *shiva* (seven days) and thirty-day periods. When news of death is received, a small cut is made in the collar, and a symbolic tear is made. The hair is not cut during this period. The mourner may keep silent, like Aaron, or he may talk and weep, whatever he or she chooses to do.

264. Tabernacle

Aaron, however, could not bear to eat the sin offering:

> 'When things like these happened
> to me, if I had eaten a sin offering
> today, would it have been good in
> the sight of the LORD?' When Moses
> heard that, it seemed good in his
> sight.[265]

Although required to maintain outward dignity because the inaugural anointing oil was still upon him, Aaron's inward, silent grief prohibited him from eating the sin offering in the holy place. Indeed, even the average Israelite had to guarantee that his Sukkot offering was not gathered while he was in a state of mourning, for it was most holy:

> I have not eaten of it while
> mourning, nor have I removed any
> of it while I was unclean, nor offered
> any of it to the dead.[266]

No matter how exalted one's position or how low, a human being's death is to be treated with respect. The dead still have a consciousness even though it is separated from the body. The spirit still belongs to the Creator. Aaron was allowed to mourn silently for his sons and skip eating the sin offering. Moses ensured that Aaron's sons would be mourned properly by all Israel:

> But your kinsmen, the whole house of
> Israel, shall bewail the burning which
> the LORD has brought about.

Mourning and respectful burial is an important obligation of the living to the dead. These essential courtesies of death help the mourner to complete the seven-day and thirty-day periods of mourning that help him or her to move to less soul-intensive periods of grief in a healthy way. Going on as

265. Le 10:19-20

266. Dt 26:14

if nothing happened is not an option. The soul (*nefesh*) is appetites, emotions, desires, and intellect. Because it is the life-force[267] of a human being, it is most powerful in controlling human behavior, and one spends a lifetime teaching the nefesh to yield to the authority of the *ruach* (spirit).

The Father in Heaven created human beings; therefore, He established ways of addressing the power of the soul, even in mourning. Grief is an emotion so powerful that it does overpower everything else for a period. This is why one cannot gather his Sukkot tithe in a state of mourning. It overpowers the intended spiritual benefit of preparing to rejoice with it. Uncontrolled grief can take over life and steal away the intended vitality and joy of being human.

It can also cause distress to the very deceased over which one mourns excessively, who, according to Yeshua's Rich Man/Lazarus parable,[268] still has an awareness or consciousness of his family on earth. When the living persist in transgressions, the dead may be aware of it. The best memorial for the dead is to live a life of spiritual, Word-obedient transformation. The deceased are not pleased with tattoos, séances, or drunken parties to celebrate their lives. They do not want to be asked to take the place of Yeshua as an intercessor for sins.

Mourning, crying, remaining silent, or speaking warmly of the deceased? Yes. Scripture establishes these things. Remembering aloud their acts of faith? Yes. Scripture establishes these things.

Grief must be given control for a defined period of mourning, and then it is gradually quieted "like a weaned child."[269] The memories, and even the regrets, become part of personal growth and inner contemplation. Ironically, once the grief begins to function in its defined role, even bitter memories can be sweetened over time. In the grief, the individual

267. the life [*nefesh*] is in the blood

268. Lk 16:19-31

269. Ps 131:2

searches for answers, and in many cases, there are no answers. Given time, however, questions about the deceased person's life, and even mode or time of death, is answered within. It is not so much a conscious resolution, but one understood at the higher level of the spirit, or *neshamah*.

One way of remembering the dead is to say Kaddish in their honor, which is a prayer, for up to a year after their passing. It is the Jewish way of saying as did Job,

> Naked I came from my mother's womb, And naked I shall return there. The LORD gave and the LORD has taken away. Blessed be the name of the LORD.[270]

A form of the prayer goes like this in English:

> Magnified and sanctified be His great name in the world which He has created according to His will. May He establish His kingdom during your life and during your days, and during the life of the whole house of Israel, even swiftly and soon, and say amen.

> Let His great name be blessed forever and to all eternity.

> Blessed, praised, and glorified, exalted, extolled and honored, magnified and lauded is the Name of the Holy One, blessed is He, though He is high above all the blessings and songs, praises and consolations which are uttered in the world. And say amen.

270. Job 1:21

> May He Who makes peace in His

high places make peace upon us
and upon all Israel, and say amen.

Saying Kaddish to honor the memory of the dead is very emotionally intense in the first days and weeks. Over the passing months, the mourner notices that there is still a catch in the heart or moisture in the eyes, but gradually a sweet sorrow fills in the places of the horrible pain and void. The Ruach HaKodesh (Holy Spirit) stitches those torn places from where the loved one's presence has been ripped in the soul.

There are significant passages in the Kaddish that sanctify the Name of the Holy One:

Magnified and sanctified be *His great Name* in the world which He has created according to His will...

Blessed, praised, and glorified, exalted, extolled and honored, magnified and lauded *is the Name of the Holy One*...

When one reads the Kaddish prayer, it is not easy at first to see what such a prayer glorifying the Father has to do with comfort for the loss of a loved one. One's response to a death, however, can indeed sanctify the Holy One as the prayers above state. To find the connection, it can be beneficial to examine what happens when proper mourning does *not* occur for a beloved family member or national leader. The Kaddish is another form of a Hebrew root word meaning holiness, *kadash*. In Exodus 20, the Israelites camped at Kadesh, a place where the Name should have been held up as holy, *kadosh*.

Something horrible happened there, though:

Then the sons of Israel, the whole
congregation, came to *the
wilderness of Zin in the first month*;
and the people stayed at *Kadesh*.
Now *Miriam died there and was*

buried there. There was no water
for the congregation, and they
assembled themselves against
Moses and Aaron.

What is missing between "...buried there." and "There
was no water..."? Mourning! Why were the people
not given thirty days of mourning for one of their
leaders? Miriam was a national leader and comfort
to the nascent nation of Israel. "All the women
followed her."[271] In fact, the sages say that Adonai
gave the manna in the merit of Moses's faithfulness,
the pillar of cloud in the merit of Aaron, and the
rock of water in the merit of Miriam. An ancient
synagogue mosaic pictures Miriam's rock streaming
water to the encampments of each of the twelve
tribes. This, the Jewish sages say, is why the water
dried up after Miriam's death when it had flown so
freely on their journeys. Miriam was a comforter,
teacher, and praise leader to her people:

> Indeed, I brought you up from the
> land of Egypt and ransomed you
> from the house of slavery, *and I
> sent before you Moses, Aaron and
> Miriam.*[272]

Why would Moses and Aaron neglect to mourn and
call all Israel to mourn for her passing? Instead of
comforting the grieving Israelites who lost a spiritual
mother, why did they call them names, "You rebels...
shall WE bring forth water from this rock...?" Think
of the significance of that rock. Yeshua was the
manna; Yeshua was the Angel of the Presence in
the pillar of cloud (in whom was the Sacred Name);
Yeshua was the Rock of water. All three leaders in
Israel were living prophecies of Yeshua, who supplied
every need.

271. Ex 15:20 Did it make sense, then, to become angry and to strike
the Rock TWICE in front of the whole congregation?
272. Micah 6:4 Miriam's memory and the sin of Moses and Aaron

are related. After all, Moses and Aaron knew and taught mourning rituals to Israel, which for them, dated as far back as Sarah, whom Abraham buried and mourned. Moses and Aaron had the honor of mourning rituals after their deaths, so did Nadab and Avihu, even though all Israel had to perform the rituals on Aaron's behalf:

> When all the congregation saw that Aaron had died, all the house of Israel wept for Aaron thirty days.[273]

> Although Moses was one hundred and twenty years old when he died, his eye was not dim, nor his vigor abated. So the sons of Israel wept for Moses in the plains of Moab thirty days; then the days of weeping and mourning for Moses came to an end.[274]

Aaron and Moses were honored with national mourning, even Nadab and Avihu after they offered strange fire, but not Miriam. This was not just a horrible oversight, dishonoring the work and memory of Miriam, it was a failure to regard the Rock as Holy. Moses and Aaron said, "Shall WE bring forth water from this rock...?" What came forth was not the comforting waters of Miriam, but the controversial (Meribah), tumultuous waters of unbridled emotion.

When we do not allow ourselves to mourn, those powerful emotions will manifest themselves eventually. It may be through anger, depression, irritability, hyper-sensitivity, or any number of emotions for which we cannot exactly find a reason. When a loved one dies, mourn. Mourn appropriately, but mourn. Honor the memory, for within each human being is some spark of our Creator. Even honor the corpse with proper handling and burial, for one contextual definition of a "Philistine" in Scripture is a "corpse abuser."

273. Ex 20:29

274. Dt 34:7-8

What if that close relative was exceedingly wicked and mistreated you horribly? Again, there was some spark of the Creator in that person. Mourn that the tiny spark of holiness was removed from the world, even if it feels impossible to mourn for the person. Mourn that the great potential of a human being was largely wasted and the opportunities lost.

When one reads the Kaddish prayer, it is not easy at first to see what such a prayer glorifying the Father has to do with comfort of the loss of a loved one.

> ...blessed is He, though He is high
> above all the blessings and songs,
> praises *and consolations* which are
> uttered in the world...

Taking into context Miriam's dishonorable farewell from her two brothers, it begins to make sense. Yes, The Holy One IS high above all blessings, songs, praises, *and consolations* uttered in the world, but why do it anyway? Miriam was a blessing and a praise song to Israel and from Israel to The Holy One. She echoed Moses' Song at the Sea! Consolations should have been uttered at her death, but instead Moses and Aaron respond with words like, "You rebels!" This is a play-on word in Hebrew, for the root of Miriam's name, *marah*, means rebellion or bitterness.

If, as Yeshua taught in his parable, the dead still have a consciousness of their family on earth, then what must Miriam have thought while she made her post-mortem journey with the angels? Why did her brothers and the nation not help her to cross over to her resting place of comfort with Father Abraham? No wonder Yeshua says, "Woman, why are you weeping?" and "Miriam!" when Miriam Magdelene sees him in the garden after the resurrection. What a beautiful reminder to the readers of the Gospel of John!

The waters of Gan Eden in Genesis Two are described as "giving drink to the whole Garden." In John 7:38, Yeshua identified himself as these living waters who gave drink at the Feast of Sukkot. Miriam's role within Israel was to be a comforter, a prophetess who encouraged the Israelites that they could eventually return to the Garden, symbolized by going into the Promised Land. For this reason, she deserved honor because of the well, for she prophesied of Yeshua's work to cleanse mankind from his own corpse of sin that prevented him from returning to the Garden. Now it makes sense why it was such a grave error for Moses and Aaron not to honor her in death, not just as a close family member, but a prophetess.

There is a Torah portion called "Chukkat," which explains the process for mixing water and ashes of the red heifer in order to sprinkle those who have come into contact with a corpse. According to the Jewish Midrash, Miriam's well was twelve streams of water, one for each tribe. The water gushed forth from the well and filled the twelve streams, and then it flowed to all sides for the 600,000 people to draw water.

Chukkat, specifically Numbers 21:16, describes the 40th year of being in the desert before entering the land of Israel:

> And from thence to Be'er; that is
> the well whereof the LORD said unto
> Moses: 'Gather the people together,
> and I will give them water.'[275]

Israel journeyed to a place called Be'er – באר. In Hebrew, a be'er is a well. Orly (2018) writes concerning this verse in Chukkat:

> Notice an interesting phenomenon about this word:

וּמִשָּׁם, **בְּאֵרָה: הוּא הַבְּאֵר**, אֲשֶׁר אָמַר יְהוָה לְמֹשֶׁה, אֱסֹף אֶת-הָעָם, וְאֶתְּנָה לָהֶם מָיִם

275. Nu 21:16

At the beginning of the verse, the word Be'er in Hebrew is spelled with the letter 'Heh' at the end בְּאֵרָה - Be'erah. This could mean 'to/ toward Be'er,' similarly to 'HA'BAITAH' - הביתה - to the house. But on the other hand, it may allude to the feminine aspect of the well by having the letter ה 'Hey' at the end of this word. This is especially striking since the verse continues with:

"...that is the well..." הוא הַבְּאֵר

Here the word באר is preceded by the masculine הוא (he) but the vowels make it be pronounced as היא (she), since there is the "ee" sound ('hirik' vowel) under the first letter ה.

To simplify Orly's explanation of the grammar and spelling for those who can't read the Hebrew letters, the well is described in the verse using both female and male gender! This does not introduce gender confusion, but prophetic applications that shed light on why the well was attributed to Miriam's prophetic work within Israel.

16

ENOCH AND ELIJAH

The rabbinic traditions concerning Enoch and Elijah shed some light on the resurrection, the ishim, and how resurrected human beings fit into the picture. According to rabbinic tradition, the Shunnamite's son was young Jonah, whom Yeshua cites as an example of his own resurrection time frame. For a Jewish audience, Yeshua would also have been making a reference to someone who had been resurrected before, so the "sign of Jonah" is both resurrection and three days/three nights.

The judgment of the resurrected dead is another topic for another book, but for now, it suffices to understand Yeshua's statement that the righteous will be like angels, or ishim after resurrection, not like Jonah, who would have died again. A transformation is coming.

Although Scripture does document other resurrections, such as Lazarus or the Shunnamite's son, two Biblical figures did not die in the way humans normally do, nor did they resurrect to a physical body like Lazarus or Jonah. Enoch and Elijah were "taken" because they walked with God. Elijah received curbside service from the chariots of Israel, which represents the warrior aspect of angelic beings.

Miriam prophesied of the heavenly chariots' victory over death by singing about the chariots of Pharaoh, who represented the ruler over Hades, or Abaddon.[276] Heavenly chariots accompany those "taken" into the heavenlies:

> Miriam the prophetess, Aaron's sister, took the timbrel in her hand, and all the women went out after her with timbrels and with dancing. Miriam answered them, 'Sing to the Lord, for He is highly exalted; the horse and his rider He has hurled into the sea.'[277]

In Hebrew, there is no differentiation between the driver of a horse or the rider of a horse, and in the Book of Revelation, the four destructive riders are released to bring judgment to the earth. To the righteous resurrected, they will have no destroying power, for they will have been surrounded by the chariots of Israel:

> Elisha saw it and cried out, 'My father, my father, the chariots of Israel and its horsemen!' And he saw Elijah no more. Then he took hold of his own clothes and tore them in two pieces.[278]

After Elisha takes Elijah's prophetic mantle, he also tells his servant, who is frightened by enemy chariots, to observe the warrior chariots of Heaven:

> Then Elisha prayed and said, 'O LORD, I pray, open his eyes that he may see.' And the LORD opened the servant's eyes and he saw; and behold, the mountain was full of horses and chariots of fire all around Elisha.[279]

These fiery chariots transport the righteous dead to a different realm. According to rabbinic tradition, Enoch and Elijah became ishim, and both appear

276. Pharaoh's servants said to him, "How long will this man be a snare to us? Let the men go, that they may serve the Lord their God. Do you not realize that Egypt is *destroyed*?" (Ex 10:7) "Destroyed" is *avdah*, from the same Hebrew root as the noun construct for the place-name *Abaddon*.

277. Ex 15:20-21

278. 2 Ki 2:12

279. 2 Ki 6:17

in Jewish expectation of apocalyptic events in the *Brit HaChadasha* (New Testament). Both figure prominently in the defeat of The Assyrian, a type of antichrist, by the Seven Shepherds and the Eight Princes of Men according to Jewish expectation as recorded in Hanukkah liturgy.

Enoch's genealogy holds a clue. He was the seventh from Adam, and his name in Hebrew, *Chanokh*, has the same root as Chanukkah, the eight-day Feast of Dedication. *The Seven Shepherds: Hanukkah in Prophecy* gives more detailed information about their roles in the end times. Seven is a number of completion, and eight is a number of new beginnings, especially transformation from natural to supernatural. Jewish tradition speaks of higher heavens, and although Scripture provides no information about a seventh or eighth Heaven, it does specify the third Heaven as "Paradise," also known as *Gan Eden*, the Garden of Eden:

> I know a man in Christ who fourteen years ago—whether in the body I do not know, or out of the body I do not know, God knows—such a man was caught up to *the third heaven*. And I know how such a man—whether in the body or apart from the body I do not know, God knows— was caught up *into Paradise* and heard inexpressible words, which a man is not permitted to speak.[280]

Paradise is directly related to *Gan Eden*, or the Garden of Eden. When Paul describes the experience, he is unsure whether the "man," whom we know from other Scriptures is Paul himself, was in or out of his natural body. He does go "up," so he ascends into the third heaven of Paradise, Gan Eden.

One piece of traditional lore that may help the reader visualize "going up" is that of Adam and Eve

280. 2 Co 12:2-4

in Gan Eden. It is believed that when they fell in sin, they descended spiritually. Prior to the fall, they had garments of light, and after the fall, they were given animal-like skins as described in (Ge 3:21). In the perception of the commentators, a descending could be spiritual, so an ascending also could be spiritual.

> For the body of man is only a garment. However, his ability to feel pleasure and pain lives on, even after the covering has been stripped off.[281]

Try to think beyond the natural directions of up and down, and think spiritually in the different levels of Heaven viewed by Paul in his vision. To experience any realm of the Kingdom of Heaven greater than the natural earth is to ascend, yet the dead descend to Sheol. Each represents a better level than the last, so Jacob's ladder makes sense. He saw the angels of God ascending and descending to earth at Beit El, which he names the "House of God." Angels don't literally need to use a ladder to go up and down, but the description of a human ladder helps the reader understand that the angels were going up and down, passing into and out of different realms of the Kingdom of Heaven.

Likewise, the building of the Tabernacle and the Temple were to elevate the nation of Israel spiritually, and they in turn were to elevate the nations spiritually, each experiencing something of a better Kingdom than fallen earth in their worship. Examine the many statements Yeshua makes concerning the Kingdom of Heaven, and there is a pattern. Yeshua believes the Kingdom is "at hand." It is very close. Something that is "at hand" can almost be touched or can be touched.

281. Salanter, 2004, p. 95

Another phrase Yeshua uses repeatedly in reference to the Kingdom of Heaven is "enter." Although the

Kingdom of Heaven is already "at hand" for human beings and "within you," they still must "enter" it, and it is only entered with righteousness that exceeds that of the Pharisees'! That righteousness must be Yeshua's righteousness, both outer and inner righteousness, depending upon Yeshua's sacrifice to transform the heart to match outer deeds of obedience. In the New Covenant, Yeshua writes the Word on hearts to propel a human being toward the righteousness necessary to enter the Kingdom of Heaven and ascend.

How does burial place of the patriarchs and matriarchs relate to entering this Kingdom of Heaven? Yeshua offers a statement that is rather oblique without the Jewish context of those couples' burial at the entrance back to Gan Eden. Yeshua says,

> I say to you that many will come
> from east and west, and recline at
> the table with Abraham, Isaac and
> Jacob in the kingdom of heaven;[282]

Yeshua makes this statement of inclusion, teaching that there is a heart-righteousness that does not depend upon one's physical pedigree, but the willing response to the Holy Spirit to hear and obey the Word. In such a case, the righteous dead will not only enter the Kingdom of Heaven, they will dine on the many dainties expected to stream through and grow in Gan Eden.

The fact that they will dine with Abraham, Isaac, and Jacob who were buried at the Garden's gateway is Yeshua's proof that those from "east and west" have a place in the Garden and recline. Reclining is a First Century posture of wealth and freedom, for the wealthy reclined as they ate, and at the annual Passover meal, all Jews recline as they eat, signifying the richness with which the Father brought them out of Egypt to be free.

282. Mt 8:11

17

HOW HIGH WILL WE FLY?

When one ascends in the Presence "with the Lord" at the shout and voice of the archangel, this ascension is not described as occurring in a dimension lacking oxygen.[283] It could describe a spiritual ascension beyond the limited area of the fallen, physical body. The incense of the saints goes "up," yet how far?

In Judges, Manoah and his wife offer a sacrifice when they receive the news that they will bear a son, Samson. The angel who delivers the news goes up in smoky flames as they watch. Consider how smoke dissipates. To the human eye, ascending to the realm of Gan Eden or the heavens inhabited by angels could be similar. At first, the smoke has formation, and as it rises, it evaporates from human sight, yet the odor of its presence lingers long after it dissipates. Likewise, an angel disappears in altar fire:

> So Manoah took the young goat with the grain offering and offered it on the rock to the LORD, and He performed wonders while Manoah and his wife looked on. For it came about when the flame went up from the altar toward heaven, that the angel of the LORD *ascended in the*

283. 1 Thessalonians 4:16 describes the saints as being caught up in the "aer." Aer, in Greek, is air in which one breathes normally.

185

flame of the altar. When Manoah and his wife saw this, they fell on their faces to the ground.[284]

284. Judges 13:19-20

285. Re 6:9

286. The Song of Moses in Dt 32:43 promises that the blood of Adonai's servants will be avenged on their enemies.

287, Psalm 47:5 says that the Lord, the King, also *ascends* with a shout. It is possible that both descending and ascending trigger a "shout" of announcement that He is crossing from realm to realm and subduing the earthly realm. Numbers 23:21 also attributes a shout to the King. The shout that accompanied the falling walls of Jericho announced the demise of the dark forces occupying the Promised Land and the arrival of a new King of Kings.

This is quite fantastic, yet the angel did not disappear and ascend into the stratosphere, but from the highest point of flame. The righteous souls "under the altar" in Revelation cry out, "How long, O Lord...?"[285] They cry out for the resurrection, which can only take place when the entire Body of Messiah is prepared to ascend. In the meantime, these souls are separate from their bodies. They are in a safe place, under the holy altar, but they long for their blood[286] to be avenged on the earth. Until the last soul is brought in and final judgment begins, their bodies cannot be transformed. The souls long for that day so that they at last can acquire the bodies and robes of light in Gan Eden to prepare for the next ascension to the Father.

According to the Jewish tradition in sources such as *Genesis Rabbah* and *Leviticus Rabbah*, the human soul (*nefesh*) remains in close proximity to the body for up to three days trying to re-enter it. After that, when the reluctant soul sees serious decomposition of its former home, it departs with the angel sent to collect it. Yeshua's resurrection of Lazarus occurred after this milestone had been passed, so it was remarkable to Jews that Yeshua could call forth the body after the serious stink had set in.

A turn of phrase in John 11:43 (KJV) is "And when he thus had spoken, he cried with a loud voice, Lazarus, come forth." The "loud voice" is operative at the resurrection in 1 Thessalonians 4:16 when the "Lord Himself shall descend from Heaven with a shout."[287]

Another source, *Pirke de Rabbi Eliezer*, chapter 34, comments on Ecclesiastes 12:7 that the *ruach* (spirit) returns to God who gave it once the seven days of mourning after death are completed. The difficulty, the rabbis posit, is when one is excessively attached to the mortal world. This attachment is formed by emphasizing accolades, pleasures, or attention gained by activities that reflect where one's true faith lies. Those will vaporize upon death, and the soul will have grown too attached to its body to turn loose gladly as the righteous will. One ancient description of how easy it is for a righteous soul to be harvested from its body by the assigned angel is "no more difficult than plucking a hair from the surface of milk."

One ancient rabbi spoke of the Garden of Eden as "upside down." Asked to explain, he said that what is important on earth is of little importance after death. What was deemed negligible on earth is given great importance in the afterlife.

After this, there are all kinds of opinions about what happens next. Assuming the ruach (spirit) goes back to God, then there is no real problem. The Creator simply accepts the return "as is" from earthly use, separated from corruptible body and soul (nefesh). The body decomposes and returns to its source. The real question is what happens to the soul, or nefesh. The nefesh is a consciousness that exists beyond the grave. It is the bundle of appetites, emotions, desires, and even intellect or reasoning. This is the part of the righteous human that waits under the altar in Revelation.

A clue in Revelation is the emphasis on "The Beast" and "The Woman." The Woman Israel is virtuous, and the sign of her virtue is that her offspring keep the commandments of God and the testimony of Yeshua. The Adulterous Woman (Harlot) is her antithesis, apostate Israel who departs from the covenant of her youth.[288] The Harlot rides a scarlet beast, or commits sin, because of the desires of her nefesh.

A great Jewish sage, Ramban, says of the soul (nefesh): "It is in the soul that the impulse to do wrong

288. Pr 2:17; Ezek 16:60

begins. When a person sins, intelligence departs, and for a moment one behaves like an animal."[289] A person who spends his life submitting to his lower nature of the nefesh rather than the higher nature of Divine spirit is "riding the beast," or letting those animal impulses carry him.

The rich man in Yeshua's parable could think, worry about the future and his family, and feel a type of torment unrelated to his decaying body. This stage of death for the nefesh is called Gehenna or Gehinnom in Scripture, or sometimes Sheol and Abaddon. Even in this lower realm, the experience of the righteous person's soul is markedly different, for Lazarus is enjoying a torment-free existence on the other side of a gulf that the rich man cannot cross or understand. The rich man is conscious, but segregated and confined.

The post-mortem place of the soul called Gehenna generally goes by seven names:

- Sheol, or Grave (Ge 37:35; Jonah 2:2)
- Abbadon, or Destruction (Ps 88:12)
- Be'er Shakhat, or Corruption (Ps 16:10)
- Bor Sha'on, or the Horrible Pit;
  and Tit Ha-Yaven, or Miry Clay (Ps 40:3)
- Tzalmavet, or Shadow of Death (Ps 107:10)
- Eretz Ha-Takhtit, or Netherworld
  (Jewish tradition)
- Gehinnom, or Lamentation (a literal valley of human sacrifice near Jerusalem; used extensively in the New Testament)

289. Lieber, p. 596

290. Raphael, 2009, p. 144

291. Prayer in memorial for the dead.

According to the tradition, this torment or rectification of the nefesh goes on for up to twelve months.[290] Whether these are twelve literal months, transitions, or epochs of time is up for debate, but Jews only say kaddish[291] for eleven months following the death of a loved one. It is thought to be rude to pray for the full twelve months since no one should be so evil as to require purification for the full twelve. It is likely that Catholics borrowed the idea of purgatory and praying for the dead from this tradition although it departs quite drastically from Jewish thought.

Yeshua's parable of the rich man and Lazarus is remarkably similar to Jewish thought about Gehenna:

> ...in certain cases, there were other ways of being exempted from the torments of Gehenna. For example, if a person's life was filled with suffering-*such as the case of a poor person*, one afflicted with bowel diseases, or one held in captivity by an oppressive government-then such an individual would be exempt from 'seeing the face of Gehenna.'[292]

The rich man in Yeshua's parable had a consciousness, or "seeing" of Lazarus, the poor man. He saw across a "great gulf" fixed between them: "And besides all this, between us and you there is a great gulf fixed, so that those who want to pass from here to you cannot, nor can those from there pass to us."[293] The *Pesikta Rabbati* states in 52:3:

> Why did the Holy One create Gehenna and Gan Eden? So that one can behold the other. How much space is between them? R. Yohanan said: The breadth of a wall. R. Hanina said: The breadth of a hand. But the Rabbis said: The two are right up against each other.

If accurate, the rabbinic perception is not of physical matter, but of realms that cannot be described to the human eye. This may be why Yeshua explained the realm of death in a parable, for a parable explains a spiritual concept in physical, human terms.

John's vision of the righteous, martyred souls under

292. Eruvin 41b, quoted in Raphael, 2009, p. 144

293. Lk 16:26

the altar hint that part of Yeshua's work to release the "spirits in prison" was to gather the righteous souls to the lower Gan Eden where they would await the resurrection and regathering of each individual spirit, soul, and body into the greater Body of Messiah at the shout and trumpet. This is also the Jewish view, for in the Talmud, Yevamot 57:16, is written a thought based on Isaiah 57:16:

> The Son of David will not come before all the souls in the body are completed; since it is said, 'For the spirit that wraps itself is from Me, and the souls which I have made.'

The belief is that the "return" to God "will take place when all souls reach completion. These souls are made up of past and future generations..."[294] The basis for this understanding is in Deuteronomy 30:1-4:

> So it shall be when all of these things have come upon you, the blessing and the curse which I have set before you, and you call them to mind in all nations where the LORD your God has banished you, and you return to the LORD your God and obey Him with all your heart and soul according to all that I command you today, *you and your sons*, then the LORD your God will restore you from captivity, and have compassion on you, and will gather you again from all the peoples where the LORD your God has scattered you. If your outcasts are at the ends of the earth, from there the LORD your God will gather you, and from there He will bring you back.

294. Kahn, 2002, p. 189

The gathering prophecy begins with the scattering of Israel into the nations. Next, Israel's descendants "return," but it is not as simple as a physical return to a physical place. It is a process called *teshuvah*, or turning from sin and returning to Adonai and holy behavior. Obedience with all the heart and soul. The curious turn of phrase is "you and your sons." Moses speaks to the Israelites standing in front of him and their descendants. That implies a collection of all souls. Once all those souls have returned to the covenant, *then* all Israel will be gathered to the Promised Land Israel. This is not just a random insertion of phrase, for the same inclusion of all souls is in the opening of the prophecy of Deuteronomy 29:14-15:

> *Now not with you alone* am I making this covenant and this oath, but both with those who stand here with us today in the presence of the LORD our God *and with those who are not with us here today...*

Following the Feast of Trumpets (Rosh HaShanah), or the gathering resurrection, comes Yom HaKippurim, which "seals up" the decrees of the resurrection of Rosh HaShanah.

The *Yizkor*, or Remembrance, service of Yom Kippur recalls those who have fallen asleep, and one prays that their loved ones' souls rest with the righteous souls of Abraham, Isaac, and Jacob; Sarah, Rebekah, Rachel, and Leah, as well as with the other righteous souls of men and women in the Garden of Eden.[295] There is little specific information about the Feast of Trumpets in the Torah, but "sealing" it with the Remembrance service is appropriate, for it is called a feast of remembrance:

> Also in the day of your gladness, and in your solemn days, and in the beginnings of your months, ye shall blow with the trumpets over your *burnt offerings*, and over the

295. *Artscroll Siddur*, Sefard, p. 858-861

sacrifices of your peace offerings;
that they may be to you for a
memorial before your God: I am the
LORD your God.[296]

The burnt offerings in Hebrew are the *olah*, which is a
resurrection, lifted-up offering.

Speak to the children of Israel,
saying: 'In the seventh month, on
the first day of the month, you shall
have a sabbath-rest, *a memorial
of blowing of trumpets*, a holy
convocation.'[297]

The LORD spoke to Moses, saying,
'On exactly the tenth day of
this seventh month is the day
of atonement; it shall be a holy
convocation for you, and *you shall
humble your souls* and present an
offering by fire to the LORD. You shall
not do any work on this same day,
for it is a day of atonement, to make
atonement on your behalf before
the LORD your God. If there is any
person who will not *humble himself*
on this same day, he shall be cut off
from his people. As for any person
who does any work on this same
day, that person I will destroy from
among his people. You shall do no
work at all. It is to be a perpetual
statute throughout your generations
in all your dwelling places. It is to be
a sabbath of complete rest to you,
and *you shall humble your souls*; on
the ninth of the month at evening,
from evening until evening you shall
keep your sabbath.'[298]

Humble yourselves in the sight of the

296. Nu 10:10

297. Le 23:24

298. Le 23:26-32

192

Lord, and He will *lift you up.*[299]

Yeshua and his brother James confirm the holy days of Trumpets and Yom Kippur as times of humility and ascension. The martyrs, the souls under the altar, are awaiting the season of Trumpets and Atonements to be lifted up.

A Jewish prayer of Yom Kippur for the souls of the righteous is thus:

> O merciful God, Who lives on high,
> grant proper rest *on the wings of the*
> *Divine Presence*-in the lofty levels
> of the holy and the pure ones, who
> shine like the glow of the firmament-
> for *the souls of the holy and pure*
> *ones who were killed, murdered,*
> *slaughtered, burned, drowned and*
> *strangled for the holiness of the*
> *Name...May their resting place be in*
> *the Garden of Eden*-therefore may
> the Master of mercy *cover them in*
> *the shelter of His wings* forever; and
> may He bind their souls in the Bond
> of Life. Hashem is their inheritance,
> and may they rest in peace on their
> resting places...

According to the Artscroll siddur, "On the wings of the Divine Presence" denotes spiritual elevation, while "under His wings" refers to Divine Protection. The souls under the altar in Revelation are already under Divine protection of the Messiah in the "Bird's Nest," yet they want to ascend to the Father in the Upper Garden with a resurrected body "on the wings" of Messiah. For this, they await the first resurrection.

Most English Bibles with subtitles will label this section of Scripture as "Martyrs":

> When He opened the fifth seal, I saw

299. Ja 4:10

193

under the altar the souls of those
who had been slain for the word of
God and for the testimony which
they held. And they cried with a
loud voice, saying, 'How long, O
Lord, holy and true, until You judge
and avenge our blood on those
who dwell on the earth?' Then a
white robe was given to each of
them; and it was said to them that
they should rest a little while longer,
until both the number of their fellow
servants and their brethren, who
would be killed as they were, was
completed.[300]

What follows the Feast of Trumpets memorial
gathering is ten days of final gathering until the
closing of the gates of repentance and the sealing
up of the martyrs at Yom Kippur's Yizkor. Here are
some passages from the Yom Kippur Yizkor service:

May the LORD remember the souls
of the holy and pure ones who
were killed, murdered, slaughtered,
burned, drowned, and strangled
for the sanctification of the Name,
because, without making a vow, I
shall give to charity on their behalf.

As reward for this, may their souls be
bound in the Bond of Life, together
with the souls of Abraham, Isaac,
and Jacob; Sarah, Rebecca,
Rachel, and Leah; and together with
the other righteous men and women
in the Garden of Eden.

These prayers make sense, for ten days after Rosh
HaShanah is the opening of the Sixth Seal, which
represents Yom Kippur, also the sixth feast of Israel.
When those Yom Kippur gates close, the wrath of the

300. Re 6:9-11

Lamb begins for the unrepentant, who are described as "late figs":

> I looked when He opened the sixth
> seal, and behold, there was a great
> earthquake; and the sun became
> black as sackcloth of hair, and the
> moon became like blood. And the
> stars of heaven fell to the earth, as
> a fig tree drops its late figs when it
> is shaken by a mighty wind. Then
> the sky receded as a scroll when
> it is rolled up, and every mountain
> and island was moved out of its
> place. And the kings of the earth,
> the great men, the rich men, the
> commanders, the mighty men,
> every slave and every free man, hid
> themselves in the caves and in the
> rocks of the mountains, and said to
> the mountains and rocks, "Fall on
> us and hide us from the face of Him
> who sits on the throne and from the
> wrath of the Lamb! For the great day
> of His wrath has come, and who is
> able to stand?"[301]

The late figs are smaller and less vigorous than the first crop. Like human beings who squander time chasing after those worldly "upside down" things, the late figs did not form a strong attachment to the Tree of Life. When a strong autumn wind comes, they'll be blown away with the fig leaves. The sky recedes like a scroll when it is rolled up, suggesting that the last words of the Torah have been read in their cycle. The Book of Deuteronomy activates 98 curses on the unrepentant. Those curses must be completed, and the scroll is rolled up and must be re-rolled to the beginning.

In the Book of Numbers, evil Balak "stood" by his *olah*, resurrection offerings, but when the Wrath

301. Re 6:12-17

of the Lamb begins, no one can stand or ascend beside an altar of unrepentant evil.

Following the purging of evil from the soul, it ascends to Gan Eden, or the Lower Garden.[302]

> But we do not want you to be uninformed, brethren, about those who are asleep, so that you will not grieve as do the rest who have no hope. For if we believe that Jesus died and rose again, even so God will bring with Him those who have fallen asleep in Jesus. For this we say to you by the word of the Lord, that we who are alive and remain until the coming of the Lord, will not precede those who have fallen asleep. For the Lord Himself will descend from heaven with a shout, with the voice of the archangel and with the trumpet of God, and the dead in Christ will rise first. Then we who are alive and remain will be caught up together with them in the clouds to meet the Lord in the air, and so we shall always be with the Lord. Therefore comfort one another with these words. (1 Th 4:1-18)

If the righteous dead are already in Gan Eden, such as the thief whose repentant faith was rewarded with Paradise by Yeshua on the cross, then this explains Paul's statement to the Thessalonians. Those who are "alive and remain" cannot precede those who are "asleep." It is only the body that is asleep, but the spirit and soul are very much alive, awaiting the awakening of the body. The spirit and soul are "wakeful, watchful," just as the golden menorah almond (*sheked*- wakeful; fix one's attention) blossoms symbolize those who resurrect to life. Those souls have been watchful over the Light

302. Raphael, p. 145

196

of the Torah and offered themselves as lamps for the commandments of God.[303]

One may compare the sleep of death to dreaming. The subconscious, which is suppressed during the day and bombarded with sensory noise, is allowed to speak. The prophets of Scripture often received prophecy in dreams and visions. The Jewish sages say that sleep is like 1/60 of death. A strange thought, no doubt, but it helps to frame what sleep is. Yeshua taught in a parable that consciousness exists even in death sleep.

Sleep is not unconsciousness at every level; the brain is alive and active, processing events and defragmenting. To an extent, it is thinking, but thinking at a more spiritual level, referred to as the neshamah. The neshamah is sometimes used interchangeably in Scripture with the ruach, or spirit. While the body is generally unresponsive to these activities, (although sleepwalking, talking, or body movement can result), everyone understands how vivid and real dreams are. Although a person perceives a dream as long or recurring throughout the night, scientists who measure brainwaves say that a dream lasts only milliseconds!

Perhaps what the sages are saying is that the experience of dreaming is a tiny taste of what consciousness is like in death. We can feel, think, see, hear, and taste, but without the cooperation of the physical body. Because of this, the rich man in the parable thirsted for a drop of water on his tongue even though he had no tongue. It was a torment of soul-thirst, describing what it is like to be separated from the Rivers of Eden and rivers of living water, the Holy Spirit.

In dreams, one often feels trapped, unable to make the body respond by screaming, running, or other actions. Sometimes one is helpless from stopping the dream from replaying. Those "asleep" in Yeshua

303. Pr 6:23

may be able to experience this state of liveliness without the feeling of helplessness, for those deemed righteous are clothed by the escorting angel in a "robe" that suffices for a corporeal form until the resurrection.

Without the "form" that takes the place of the body post-mortem, a gift to the righteous dead, a wicked person experiences the sleep of death like their idols, which ultimately is ruling one's life according to self-will instead of God's will. The idols of ancient times were merely beings exhibiting the same qualities as human beings with all their evil and good, yet given superpowers like comic book heroes:

> Their idols are silver and gold,
> The work of man's hands. They have
> mouths, but they cannot speak;
> They have eyes, but they cannot
> see; They have ears, but they cannot
> hear; They have noses, but they
> cannot smell; They have hands, but
> they cannot feel; They have feet,
> but they cannot walk; They cannot
> make a sound with their throat.
> Those who make them will become
> like them, Everyone who trusts in
> them.[304]

Idolatry is self-worship, for the gods are mere images of mankind: petty, jealous, promiscuous, scheming, greedy, and never appeased. To worship one's own soul desires, whether in the form of actual formed images or allowing the soul appetites to rule one's spirit, is idolatry. The wicked human in death experiences the soul's unrequited consciousness, yet without a form to satisfy all those urges. A wicked dead soul realizes that because of his self-worship, he gave temporary use of a human body to demons. Apart from his cooperation, those demons were only disembodied beings, unable to experience physical earth without a host. Now the wicked person has

304. Ps 115:4-8

198

become like them.

At the shout that heralds movement between the realms of Gan Eden and fallen earth, the dead "in Christ" will rise first because their spirits and souls are already in Gan Eden. This is consistent with the rabbinic expectation that at the end of days there is a collective resurrection of both a body and soul of the dead.[305] The transformed bodies of light will ascend first to reunite with soul and spirit in the Garden. As the Lord "descends" with a shout for those who are alive and remain, they too, ascend into Gan Eden to join the righteous with transformed bodies. Perhaps those who are alive at the resurrection need less time for a body transformation because there is more to work with, so they follow those who were already asleep.

There is much more to say about the many "rooms" to which one may be assigned at this stage, but it is impossible to cover everything. Perhaps the rabbinic speculation in the Midrash on Psalms 11:7 of seven classes within Gan Eden will help the reader to visualize it:

- the first class sits in the company of the King and beholds His presence
- the second dwells in the house of the King
- the third ascends to the hill to meet the King
- the fourth is in the court of the King
- the fifth is in the Tabernacle of the King
- the sixth is in the holy hill of the King
- the seventh is in the palace of the King

These are cryptic descriptions, but other sources give more vivid descriptions. Raphael records from *Yalkut Shimoni*, Bereishit 20[306] a beautiful picture of Gan Eden. When the righteous dead arrives, he is given a white robe of the clouds of glory, and on his head two crowns are placed, one of gold and one of gems and pearls. Eight myrtles are placed in his hand and he is told to go eat his food in joy. He

305. Raphael, p. 162

306. p. 153-154

goes to a place filled with brooks and eight hundred varieties of roses and myrtles.

Each person has a chamber according to the level of honor, and there are rivers of wine, milk, balsam, and honey. There are many species of trees in every corner of Gan Eden, and the Tree of Life is in its center with its branches covering the entire Garden. Above the Tree of Life is the clouds of glory, and it gives off a perfume throughout the Garden. There are seven dwelling places listed in the *Seder Gan Eden*, and in each there is a righteous woman who teaches the Torah: Batyah, daughter of Pharaoh, Yocheved, mother of Moses, Miriam, sister of Moses, Huldah the Prophetess, Abigail, David's wife, and beyond this point, the matriarchs, Sarah, Rebecca, Rachel, and Leah.[307]

In one source, those who enter Gan Eden go through four transformations through their learning experience. Upon entry, the righteous individual is changed into a child and tastes the joys of childhood.[308] This correlates with Yeshua's statement to his disciples:

307. "When the Torah was first given, Jewish tradition says it was taught to the women first. It is written, 'Thus shall you say to the house of Jacob' – the women – 'and tell the sons of Israel' (Exodus 19:3)." (Kaplan, p. 59)

308. Raphael, p. 187

309. Mk 10:13-16

And they were bringing children to Him so that He might touch them; but the disciples rebuked them. But when Jesus saw this, He was indignant and said to them, 'Permit the children to come to Me; do not hinder them; for the kingdom of God belongs to such as these. Truly I say to you, whoever does not receive the kingdom of God like a child will not enter it at all.' And He took them in His arms and began blessing them, laying His hands on them.[309]

In another passage, Yeshua's statement is equally strong:

> Truly I say to you, unless you are
> converted and become like
> children, you will not enter the
> kingdom of heaven[310]

The four transformations expected in Judaism have much validity when viewed relative to Yeshua's teaching about how one enters the Kingdom. There are three more transformations associated with Gan Eden that represent the natural stages of human life, yet it is the positive attributes of those stages emphasized, not the negative ones. For instance, old age is not a time of senility and feebleness, but of the glory of wisdom attained. The three transformations expected in the Garden are childhood, young adulthood, adulthood, and old age.

The moral of this story? No matter what an individual *thinks* he knows about Scripture, he must have the humility of a child to enter this Garden and to be instructed as if he knew nothing.

As a holding place until the resurrection, Jewish tradition speaks of the "bundle of life" for the righteous, which is taken from 1 Samuel 25:29. This bundle of righteous souls is held in safekeeping under the Throne of Glory. It is uncertain how this holding pattern bundle of living souls relates to the holding pattern of Gan Eden, unless somehow the lower Garden is located beneath the Throne of Glory.

310. Mt 18:3

18

THE RIGHTEOUS AND THE INTERMEDIATES

In Judaism, there are three classes of people at the Throne of Judgment: the righteous, the intermediates, and the wicked. Yeshua hints to these three classes in his warning to the Church of Laodicea in Revelation. The progression of judgments post-mortem is too comprehensive to address in a booklet, so for simplicity's sake, a summary of rabbinic expectation is explained in the following paragraphs. A sample from Christian literature may be read in Visions of Sadhu Sundar Singh of India, which is available to read in its entirety on multiple Christian websites. It details many parallels to the Jewish vision of the afterlife.

The righteous do not experience the torment of Sheol. They are in "Abraham's bosom" and "gathered to their people" in Gan Eden, and this is experienced immediately after death. This is distinguished from the rewards in the *Olam Haba*, or World to Come after the resurrection and Messiah's Kingdom.

The wicked and intermediates descend to Sheol. The intermediates, or "lukewarm"[311] as Yeshua calls them, are purified and experience torment for up

311. Re 3:16

to twelve months, but repentance may shorten the term. They may then ascend to Gan Eden, but

> ...their subsequent afterlife
> experience is not in any way as
> supernal and blissful as that of
> the righteous. Such sinners, even
> after they exit from Gehenna, are
> granted post-mortem repose of a
> lesser grade-that is, below that of the
> righteous-hence the phrase 'at the
> feet of the righteous.'[312]

This phrase "at the feet of the righteous" has a similar phrase in the Book of Revelation:

> He who is holy, who is true, who has
> the key of David, who opens and
> no one will shut, and who shuts and
> no one opens, says this: 'I know your
> deeds. Behold, I have put before
> you an open door which no one
> can shut, because you have a little
> power, and have kept My word, and
> have not denied My name. Behold,
> I will cause those of the synagogue
> of Satan, who say that they are Jews
> and are not, but lie—I will make
> them come and bow down at your
> feet, and make them know that I
> have loved you.[313]

It is very important for the reader to understand who the "synagogue of Satan" was in the First Century. Otherwise, the meaning of the passage will be skewed and become anti-Semitic, which neither the Father, Yeshua, nor John would tolerate. For a complete explanation of the synagogue of Satan, refer to BEKY Book, *Pharisee: Friend or Foe* by the author.

312. Raphael, pp. 266-267

313. Re 3:7-9 In a nutshell, the synagogue of Satan was specifically

the First Century Pharisaical School of Shammai, which rejected the inclusion of converts from the nations. It was called the synagogue of Satan by the Pharisaical School of Hillel, of which Paul was a member. The Hillelite Pharisaic sect embraced the Gentile convert who wanted to be included in the nation of Israel, and they rejected the pride of the Shammaiites, or the "synagogue of Satan" that would damn Gentiles eternally to Sheol. To Paul and the School of Hillel, excluding Gentile converts was a very un-Jewish position.

The hypocrisy and selfishness of those who wanted to exclude righteous Gentiles results in their Garden experience being reduced in quality. Instead of the high ("rich") position to which they believed they were entitled, the synagogue of Satan experiences a kind of poverty, or low position at the feet of those who were only apparently impoverished before death. These humble, but faithful, disciples find that once they enter the Garden, they are given the rich position to which the proud believed they would be entitled.[314] In fact, the righteous are given two crowns, one of which is mentioned in the other reference to the synagogue of Satan:

> The first and the last, who was
> dead, and has come to life, says
> this: 'I know your tribulation and
> your poverty (but you are rich),
> and the blasphemy by those who
> say they are Jews and are not, but
> are a synagogue of Satan. Do not
> fear what you are about to suffer.
> Behold, the devil is about to cast
> some of you into prison, so that you
> will be tested, and you will have
> tribulation for ten days. Be faithful
> until death, and I will give you the
> crown of life. He who has an ear, let
> him hear what the Spirit says to the
> churches.[315]

314. The reader will recall Yeshua's warning not to pick the best place at a table lest the master of the banquet move him to a lower one. Instead, one should take a lower position and allow the master to move him higher. In Luke 11:43, Yeshua addresses the Shammai mindset: "Woe to you Pharisees! For you love the best seat in the synagogues and greetings in the marketplaces." Yeshua reiterates the danger of coveting notice for one's piety and the higher position, which results in a lower position in the Kingdom. When one crowns himself on this earth, no crown remains for him in the Kingdom.

315. Re 2:8-11

Another rabbinic teaching is that "each soul experiences the state of consciousness it has evolved during the physical plane life." Yeshua makes some affirming statements concerning this belief:

> For whoever is ashamed of Me and
> My words, the Son of Man will be
> ashamed of him when He comes in
> His glory, and the glory of the Father
> and of the holy angels.[316]

This statement appears almost verbatim in Mark 8:38. Whatever belief or faith system a person has put in place prior to death, he will receive a matching reward, an existence of like kind and ironically, of his choosing.

> And I heard a voice from heaven,
> saying, "Write, 'Blessed are the dead
> who die in the Lord from now on!'"
> "Yes," says the Spirit, "so that they
> may rest from their labors, for their
> deeds follow with them."[317]

> Let the one who does wrong, still
> do wrong; and the one who is filthy,
> still be filthy; and let the one who is
> righteous, still practice righteousness;
> and the one who is holy, still keep
> himself holy. Behold, I am coming
> quickly, and My reward is with Me,
> to render to every man according to
> what he has done.[318]

This warning from John in Revelation is echoed by the Jewish sages:

316. Lu 9:26

317. Re 14:13

318. Re 22:11-12

> If a man follows a certain direction in
> this world, he will be led further in the
> same direction when he departs this
> world; as that to which he attaches
> himself in this world, so is it that to

which he will find himself attached in the other world: if holy, holy, and if defiled, defiled. If he cleaves to holiness, he will on high be drawn to that side and be made a servant to minister before The Holy One among the angels and will stand among those holy beings...similarly, if he clings here to uncleanness, he will be drawn there toward that side and be made one of the unclean company and attached to them.[319]

Presumably, anyone who was "intermediate," would need the intervention of the Spirit to break this cycle after death, which before Yeshua, was accomplished in Sheol. How Yeshua disrupted this is a matter for debate, but Yeshua does have the "key" for those who no longer desire to remain in states of filthiness. This would be an attitude of repentance, and Yeshua could advocate for this person to have an open door to enter Gan Eden for his retraining.

To the thief on the cross beside him, Yeshua promised an open door to Paradise, or Gan Eden, "this day." This promise was not based on the thief's righteous life, but Yeshua's. The thief makes a profession of guilt, which we may interpret as repentance, and then he does an accompanying deed, giving a dying man a kind word in a profession of faith when there was nothing else the thief could possibly give at that point. Only Yeshua's righteousness could open the entrance door to the Garden for the repentant thief. The other thief can represent those who "still do wrong," and proceed to punishment.

For the repentant thief or anyone else, Nachmanides describes the experience of the righteous as an elevation or ascent of the soul. They are elevated by "study, and perceive visions of God in the company of the higher beings of that place. They attain whatever [degree of] knowledge and

319. Raphael, p. 284

320. Raphael, p. 267

207

understanding created beings can achieve."[320] This explains how one that is transformed to the fourth stage of old age has attained unspeakable wisdom as well as why Paul heard things in the Third Heaven of Gan Eden that it was not permitted to utter in the lower realm of natural earth.

19

THE TUNNEL, THE LIGHT, AND BEYOND

For man goes to his eternal home while mourners go about in the street. Remember Him before the silver cord is broken and the golden bowl is crushed, the pitcher by the well is shattered and the wheel at the cistern is crushed; *then the dust will return to the earth as it was, and the spirit will return to God who gave it.*[321]

Many of those who have near-death experiences describe a tunnel and light. Even the wicked have a similar experience to young children who have not attained an age of accountability for sin, yet most describe a tunnel and light. While we've examined many sources (and there are many more to explore), most of them describe the experience of the soul after death. What happens to the *neshamah* (breath), which is sometimes used interchangeably with the *ruach* (spirit)?

The return of the neshama to "God who gave it" may explain the common experience. The spirit of

321. Ec 12:5-7

God would return to its incorruptible source. This may be experienced as being pulled through a tunnel toward a source of powerful light. That which is corruptible must go to its appropriate punishment or reward while awaiting the resurrection for final judgment. For the wicked, this would be a second death, but that second death has no power over the righteous in Gan Eden.

The Jewish mystics write that the soul enters the Lower Garden and takes on a likeness of the earthly body which is described as a luminous robe.[322] Another bit of rabbinic thought is that at the time of death, each individual is given at least a brief glimpse of the Divine Presence. This may also account for the common reported experience of glimpsing a powerful light. Continuing in the Presence, however, is dependent upon one's spiritual attainment or acceptability.

That tradition of a glimpse into the Heavenlies is matched by another tradition that describes what is known as the Evil Inclination, or the Yetzer Hara. The Evil Inclination is as the Apostle Paul described, "When I would do good, evil is present to hinder me." Each human being struggles with a natural inclination toward evil that struggles against the Spirit of Adonai. The Talmud describes the end of the Evil Inclination thus:

> In the future, the Almighty will bring the evil impulse and slay it in the presence of the righteous and the wicked. To the righteous, it will appear as a towering mountain; and to the wicked, it will appear as a strand of hair.[323]

One rabbi explained the analogy of the two perspectives. To a righteous person who, like Paul, struggled with the Evil Inclination, and who has exercised effort to overcome it, as Yeshua taught his disciples to pray, "Deliver us from the Evil....," the

322. "And there was given to each of them a white robe; and they were told that they should rest for a little while longer, until the number of their fellow servants and their brethren who were to be killed even as they had been, would be completed also." (Re 6:11)

323. Sukkah 52a

210

vanquished Evil will appear as a huge mountain because they recognize the effort and spiritual discipline it took to overcome its work in their lives.

To the wicked, it will be a source of grief, for they will see that the Evil was not so powerful as they thought. They exerted little effort to overcome it even though many transgressions were easily overcome.[324] Isaiah's oblique references to the king of Babylon and the wicked in Chapters Fourteen and Sixty-six may be hints as to the identity of this "man" who intimidated the nations with his strength, yet he is exposed in the grave as having no strength at all.

> 'For just as the new heavens and the
> new earth which I make will endure
> before Me,' declares the Lord,
> 'So your offspring and your name
> will endure. And it shall be from
> new moon to new moon and from
> sabbath to sabbath, all mankind will
> come to bow down before Me,' says
> the Lord. 'Then they will go forth and
> look on the corpses of the men who
> have transgressed against Me. For
> their worm will not die and their fire
> will not be quenched; and they will
> be an abhorrence to all mankind.'[325]

Upper Garden

Although it is not clear the sequence and relationship of the Lower Garden, the Messianic reign, Upper Garden, and the *Olam Haba* (World to Come), some information is given in Jewish tradition of the Upper Garden. In the Lower Garden, the righteous person is taught, cleansed in the waters of Gan Eden,[326] and perfumed with the spices of the plants, prepared like a bride. After completion of the purification process in the staging place of the Lower Garden, the person ascends and is given new garments necessary to experience the celestial delights of the Presence.

324. Salanter, 2004, p. 203

325. Is 66:22–24

326. For a comprehensive study of the Rivers of Eden, see *Creation Gospel Workbook Five Volume 1*.

The soul is once again immersed in the Heavenly River of Light and emerges completely purified in every aspect to approach the Presence.[327]

Post-resurrection Experience

The Scriptures and rabbinic tradition have sketched the general progression of events after death. What of the resurrection itself, though? This is where rabbinic tradition and the Newer Testament diverge, primarily in numbers. In summary, Rabbi Avraham Azulai writes in *Hesed L'Avraham 27a* (translated into English by Bar Tzadok, 1993) that:

- When Messiah comes, he will come with an ingathering of Israel's exiles to the Land of Israel
- Only 7,000 Children of Israel will be found living in the Land of Israel
- The 7,000 along with all the dead of Israel will be resurrected to life that same day into spiritual creations with spiritual bodies
- Those resurrected bodies will be like Adam's prior to sin, like Enoch's, like Moses', and like Elijah's[328]
- They shall float in the air, soaring like eagles, and all the gathered exiles will witness it
- The stone walls of Jerusalem will be destroyed and rebuilt with gems and pearls

327. Raphael, pp. 311-312

328. Enoch and Elijah were thought to have been translated into bodies of the ishim, the man-like class of angels that watch over human beings.

Yeshua and the apostles instead specifically include all righteous believers in Yeshua as taking part in the resurrection to spiritual creations. Perhaps the number 7,000 is only symbolic, but in the Scriptures cited in Section I of this booklet, the righteous dead and living who await Messiah's return will be caught up with him in the air and receive resurrected bodies. This is documented extensively by the apostles and written to be a "comfort," not a terror. In fact, John writes in Revelation that the righteous in numbers "that no one could count" include every "nation, tribe, and tongue."[329]

Revelation 20 summarizes the events following the first resurrection, which is the resurrection of the righteous. Resurrection is a whole being restored, spirit, soul, and body, although the newly-unified resurrected being is greatly transformed from the mortal life. He is "like angels." Once the first resurrection occurs, though, presumably those awaiting it in Gan Eden will receive those bodies along with those "who are alive and remain" in the earth at the resurrection.

Those who are not reckoned and gathered in the first resurrection must await a second resurrection after the 1,000-year reign of Messiah. At the conclusion of that epoch, the serpent is loosed for a little while, and it will deceive many of those alive on the earth. After a final world war, the serpent will be thrown into the abyss with the beast and the false prophet. This is when the second resurrection takes place.

What is called the Great White Throne judgment begins, and the books are opened:

> Then I saw a great white throne and Him who sat upon it, from whose presence earth and heaven fled away, and no place was found for them. And I saw the dead, the great and the small, standing before the throne, and books were opened; and another book was opened, which is the book of life; and the dead were judged from the things which were written in the books, according to their deeds. And the sea gave up the dead which were in it, and death and Hades gave up the dead which were in them; and they were judged, every one of them according to their deeds. Then death and Hades were thrown

329. Re 5:9; Re 7:9

213

into the lake of fire. This is the
second death, the lake of fire. And
if anyone's name was not found
written in the book of life, he was
thrown into the lake of fire.[330]

All those who missed the first resurrection are brought before the judge, and the books are opened. Judgments are assigned and executed according to one's deeds, and a new era begins. The era of Messiah's 1,000-year reign transforms into the era of the *Olam Haba*, or The World to Come, and New Jerusalem. At this point, John's narrative converges with Rabbi Azulai's. The city of New Jerusalem is described as having new walls. The description of gold and other precious stones is extensive in Revelation 21:10-27.

Rabbi Azulai's description of the resurrected Israelites as "soaring like eagles" matches the Israelites' experience when they departed Egypt in a type of paleo-prophecy of the resurrection:

> Moses went up to God, and the
> LORD called to him from the
> mountain, saying, "Thus you shall say
> to the house of Jacob and tell the
> sons of Israel: 'You yourselves have
> seen what I did to the Egyptians,
> and how I bore you on eagles'
> wings, and brought you to Myself.
> Now then, if you will indeed obey
> My voice and keep My covenant,
> then you shall be My own possession
> among all the peoples, for all the
> earth is Mine; and you shall be to
> Me a kingdom of priests and a holy
> nation.' These are the words that you
> shall speak to the sons of Israel."
>
> So Moses came and called the
> elders of the people, and set before

330. Re 20:11-15

them all these words which the
LORD had commanded him. All the
people answered together and said,
"All that the LORD has spoken we will
do!" And Moses brought back the
words of the people to the LORD.
The LORD said to Moses, "Behold, I
will come to you in a thick cloud, so
that the people may hear when I
speak with you and may also believe
in you forever."[331]

The context of the eagles' wings statement is the
giving of the Ten Commandments at Mount Sinai.
John prophesies that the Woman in Revelation will
be given the two wings of the great eagle. Even
John says the angel "carried me away in the Spirit
to a great and high mountain, and showed me the
holy city, Jerusalem, coming down out of heaven
from God, having the glory of God."[332]

This should call to mind the Apostle Paul's teaching
in Galatians 4:26 concerning our Mother Sarah, who
is from above, versus Hagar the slave woman from
below: "But the Jerusalem above is free; she is our
mother." Sarah above is a symbol of resurrection in
her intercession for the resurrection of Isaac and her
burial at the gateway back to Gan Eden. This leads
to a New Jerusalem for those who have part in the
first resurrection.

Another point of reference is the promise of a kingdom
priesthood to Israel. This "free" Israel was intended to
soar in the cloud like eagles, but they fell into the sin
of the Golden Calf when Moses tarried on the high
mountain. The promise of priesthood, however, had
earlier been extended to the still-soaring Israelites
above. In Revelation, the first resurrection does result
in a 1,000-year priesthood on earth:

Blessed and holy is the one who has
a part in the first resurrection; over

331. Ex 19:3-9

332. Re 21:10

215

these the second death has no power, but they will be priests of God and of Christ and will reign with Him for a thousand years.[333]

The Jewish mystical reference to Messiah's Palace as the "bird's nest,"[334] does have at least a symbolic correlation to Scriptural foundations, the rescue, and therefore resurrection, of Israel.[335]

Yeshua teaches the second resurrection in another passage:

> For just as the Father raises the dead and gives them life, even so the Son also gives life to whom He wishes. For not even the Father judges anyone, but He has given all judgment to the Son, so that all will honor the Son even as they honor the Father. He who does not honor the Son does not honor the Father who sent Him. Truly, truly, I say to you, he who hears My word, and believes Him who sent Me, has eternal life, and does not come into judgment, but has passed out of death into life.
>
> Truly, truly, I say to you, an hour is coming and now is, when the dead will hear the voice of the Son of God, and those who hear will live. For just as the Father has life in Himself, even so He gave to the Son also to have life in Himself; and He gave Him authority to execute judgment, because He is the Son of Man. Do not marvel at this; for an hour is coming, in which all who are in the tombs will hear His voice, and will come forth; those who did the good deeds to a resurrection of life, those

333. Re 20:6

334. *kan ha-tzippor*

335. Raphael, p.186

216

who committed the evil deeds to a resurrection of judgment.

The voice, Scripture and tradition establish, is the trumpet blast of Rosh Hashanah, the Feast of Trumpets. Yeshua gives a few points relevant to our study:

- Hearing and obeying the Word causes one to pass out of death and "into" life. Perhaps the phrase "enter the Kingdom of Heaven" is equivalent to going "into."
- The hour of resurrection is coming "and now is." How can this be unless Yeshua is referring to something the righteous already practice, the holy assembly of Rosh HaShanah?
- It is only those who "hear" who live. The context for "hearing" in Scripture is obeying the Word, which is found in the Israelite statement of faith and the greatest commandment[336] on which all other commandments hang: "Hear, O Israel, the LORD your God, the LORD is One."
- Yeshua implies that the "resurrection to life" is the first resurrection, and the "resurrection to judgment" is the second.

It is unfruitful to debate whether any individual "heard" and "obeyed" the Word, for Yeshua says he gives life to whomever *he* wishes! Noah was a man "righteous in his generation." Noah is not being compared to another holier generation because his was most wicked. Yeshua is given the discretion to judge a person according to the situation into which he was born and the Word available to the person.

Ishah: Woman or Wife?

> Then one of the seven angels who had the seven bowls full of the seven last plagues came and spoke

336. Loving one's neighbor is the other "peg" on which all the commandments hang.

with me, saying, 'Come here, I will show you the bride, the wife of the Lamb.'[337]

The Hebrew word *ishah* has three meanings: woman, wife, and Eve's name before Adam renamed her Chavah (Eve). Significantly, both the angels and the "gardener" in John's gospel call Mary "Ishah." A woman has an essence of fire (*esh*), either holy or adulterous:

> Can a man (*ish*) take fire (*esh*) in his bosom and his clothes not be burned?

> Or can a man walk on hot coals and his feet not be scorched? So is the one who goes in to his neighbor's wife (*eshet*);[338]

> Whoever touches her will not go unpunished.[339]

There is a play-on word with man (ish) and woman (ishah, eshet). To say "her husband" in Hebrew, one says "ishah," joining *ish* (husband) and *ah* (feminine possessive suffix). The "woman" (ishah) actually is "her husband" (ishah), and therefore the adulterer is not to separate what is one even linguistically. There is a unity and wholeness between husband and wife that should not be torn apart.

In the text of Leviticus 1:9, a wordplay demonstrates how Hebrew can embed significance into a passage. The *olah* offering is burned whole except for the skin. The skin remains on earth while the rest is completely burned up:

- He shall slay the young bull before the LORD; and Aaron's sons the priests shall offer up the blood and *sprinkle the blood around on the altar* that is at the

337. Re 21:9

338. a noun construct of *ishah*

339. Pr 6:27-29

218

doorway of the tent of meeting.[340]
- He shall then skin the burnt offering
  and cut it into its pieces.
- The sons of Aaron the priest shall put fire on
  the altar and arrange wood on the fire.
- Then Aaron's sons the priests shall arrange
  the pieces, the head and the suet over the
  wood which is on the fire that is on the altar.
- Its entrails, however, and its legs
  he shall wash with water.
- And the priest shall offer up in smoke
  all of it on the altar for a burnt offering
  (olah), an offering by fire (isheh) of
  a soothing aroma to the LORD.

Revelation 6:9-11 describes the souls under the altar who ask for their "blood" to be avenged. This blood was part of their olah offering. Their skin was "burned" and left on the earth for the resurrection. Their inner parts have been washed with water (by the Word) and then purged in fire (of the Holy Spirit). A Jewish body is prepared for burial by washing it and shrouding it. The "soothing aroma" of sacrifice is accepted in rabbinic tradition to be a physical description of the Father's pleasure when His children love Him by obeying Him.[341]

The pronunciation of Hebrew words prior to the insertion of vowels depended upon knowing the context of the word, so isheh (by fire) would have been pronounced correctly by the reader. Without the vowels, however, isheh can be pronounced ishah, a wordplay between "by fire" and "woman." Now it makes sense why a man would take hot coals in his bosom if he took another man's wife! The holy offering of obedience turns to fiery hot coals to the disobedient.

An olah offering comes from the root "to go up," "not only because it goes up in smoke but because it elevates the soul of the person who performs this

340. Le 1:5

341. Lieber, p. 589

act."[342] If we want the soul to go anywhere, it's up. The poorest person could bring only a dove for an *olah*, but reassuringly, Messiah's Palace in the Lower Garden is called The Bird's Nest.

The olah is a picture of how an individual ascends to the Garden, for the root *alah* in Strong's (H5930) is used as more than the whole burnt offering, but also as "ascent, stairway, steps." Returning to live in the Land of Israel is called *Aliyah*. Israel represents the Garden hovering just above it, but out of sight to the natural eye.

342. Lieber, p. 588

20

THE RESURRECTION OFFERING

In Section I, numerous passages in the Torah were tied to Jewish expectation concerning the resurrection. In Section II, more traditional Jewish sources intersected with Scripture. With all the interrelated themes of the resurrection and at least a general understanding of the process of death, post-mortem experience, first resurrection, the reign of Messiah, and the second resurrection, another passage of Scripture sheds light upon the ancient sacrificial altar, Isaac, and resurrection.

Here are a few Hebrew vocabulary words that enrich the connections:

> *mizbeach*
> *Kohen*
> *olah*
> *shlamim* peace offering, from same root as shalom

Leviticus painstakingly instructs Israel in the rituals of sacrifice. A particular passage, Leviticus 6:8-13 (6:1-6 in the Hebrew Bible), is an example of how the seed prophecies of the Torah teach the resurrection:

> Then the LORD spoke to Moses,

saying, 'Command Aaron and his
sons, saying, "'This is the law for the
burnt offering: the burnt offering
itself shall remain on the hearth on
the altar all night until the morning,
and the fire on the altar is to be
kept burning on it. The priest is to
put on his linen robe, and he shall
put on undergarments next to his
flesh; and he shall take up the ashes
to which the fire reduces the burnt
offering on the altar and place
them beside the altar. Then he shall
take off his garments and put on
other garments, and carry the ashes
outside the camp to a clean place.
The fire on the altar shall be kept
burning on it. It shall not go out, but
the priest shall burn wood on it every
morning; and he shall lay out the
burnt offering on it, and offer up in
smoke the fat portions of the peace
offerings on it. Fire shall be kept
burning continually on the altar; it is
not to go out.'"[343]

To more easily unpack the prophecies, it is necessary
to know that Abraham was instructed to offer Isaac
as an olah-offering, which is sometimes translated as
"whole burnt offering":

He said, 'Take now your son, your
only son, whom you love, Isaac, and
go to the land of Moriah, and offer
him there as a burnt offering (olah)
on one of the mountains of which I
will tell you.'[344]

Go back through the Leviticus passage above, and
try substituting the word "resurrection" each time
you see "burnt offering." This gives some context
of the principles of resurrection. If it's still not clear,

343. Le 6:8-13

344. Ge 22:2

222

here is a line-by-line study from a translation that preserves the transliteration of the olah offering, the altar (Mizbe'ach), and the priest (Kohen).

Leviticus Olah-offering	Commentary
Adonai spoke to Moses, saying: C o m m a n d Aaron and his sons, saying: This is the law of the olah-offering:	Aaron is noted in Judaism for his attribute of lovingkindness and willingness to intercede on behalf of the Israelites when they sinned. The service of the resurrection offering is given to a priesthood who are heirs of one known for mercy: "You have made them to be a kingdom and priests to our God; and they will reign upon the earth." (Re 5:10) The consecration "ha-mishchah" of the priests in Leviticus 8:8 is via his anointing, "yimshach."[345] The Hebrew root mashach is the root of Mashiach, or Messiah, Christ. The priests of the olah offering are a type of messiah, who also commands his children to offer themselves a living sacrifice.[346]
It is the olah-offering that remains on the flame, on the Mizbe'ach, all night until morning, and the fire of the Mizbe'ach will be kept aflame on it.	The resurrection offering endures or "stays" in the flame of the Holy Spirit on the bronze altar. The first altar fire was lit by fire from Heaven.

345. The verse numbers are slightly different in the Hebrew Bible: "Then he poured some of the anointing oil on Aaron's head and anointed him, to consecrate him. Next Moses had Aaron's sons come near and clothed them with tunics, and girded them with sashes and bound caps on them, , just as the LORD had commanded Moses (Le 8:12-13)

346. Ro 12.1

347. In *Etz Chaim* (p. 598), the commentator points out that although the Hebrew word *kipper* (as in Yom Kippur) means "to cover over, conceal," the root has an Akkadian cognate *kuppuru*, which means "to wipe off, burnish, cleanse." To the ancient Near Eastern cultures, washing a guest's feet may have had ritual symbolism, not just an obligation of hospitality. Rabbinic tradition says that obeying the commandments "burnishes" the individual and brings forth a glow of light.

The Kohen shall put on his fitted linen tunic, and he shall put on the linen Michnasaim on his flesh;	The priest puts on linen garments to tend the fire of the resurrection. John describes such a person: "I saw one like a son of man, *clothed in a robe reaching to the feet, and girded across His chest with a golden sash.* His head and His hair were white like white wool, like snow; and His eyes were like a flame of fire. His feet were like burnished[347] bronze, when it has been made to glow in a furnace... When I saw Him, *I fell at His feet like a dead man.* And He placed His right hand on me, saying, "Do not be afraid; I am the first and the last, and the living One; and *I was dead, and behold, I am alive forevermore*, and I have the keys of death and of Hades." (Re 1:13-15; 17-18)
he shall raise up the ashes which the fire will consume of the olah-offering on the Mizbe'ach, and place it next to the Mizbe'ach.	The "ashes" are the souls of the righteous that are stirred by the Kohen on the altar to consume the "beast" of the olah offering. Those ashes are placed at the base of the altar and then removed to a pure place, the Garden.

He shall remove his garments and he shall wear other garments,	The analogy is that while a servant prepares the Master's meal, he dirties his garments. When he is prepared to enter the Master's Presence to serve the meal, he changes into his best garment. Yeshua took on the earthy garment of human flesh, but he put back on the glory that was his from the beginning at the resurrection. "I saw underneath the altar the souls of those who had been slain because of the word of God, and because of the testimony which they had maintained; and they cried out with a loud voice, saying, "How long, O Lord, holy and true, will You refrain from judging and avenging our blood on those who dwell on the earth?" And there was given to each of them a white robe;[348] and they were told that they should rest for a little while longer, until the number of their fellow servants and their brethren who were to be killed even as they had been, would be completed also." (Re 6:9-11) Those who await the rest of the righteous to be added for the first resurrection are given robes of light while they wait.

348. Raphael quotes: "When the time comes for the spirit to leave this world... it cannot do so until the Angel of Death has taken off the garment of this body. When that has been done he again puts on that other garment in Gan Eden of which he had to divest himself when he entered this world. And the whole joy of the spirit is in that celestial body." (p. 297)

and he shall take the ashes outside of the camp, to a pure place.	Once the righteous die, their "ashes," symbolizing the purified soul, are removed to the Lower Garden, a pure place to await resurrection.
The fire on the Mizbe'ach shall remain aflame on it, it shall not be extinguished; and the Kohen shall light wood upon it every morning;	The purification of the saints is an ongoing, daily process. The wood is kindled every morning with a chance to offer one's self as a living sacrifice, holy and acceptable. Because the Kohen Yeshua is a merciful high priest, his mercies are new every morning.
he shall arrange the olah-offering on it and shall make the fats of the peace-offering to go up in smoke.	The continual burnt offering of the morning sacrifice is followed by the evening sacrifice. There is a first and second resurrection: "The rest of the dead did not come to life until the thousand years were completed. This is the first resurrection." (Re 20:5) Along with the resurrection offering, a peace-offering, or *shlamim* goes up with it. This is not only a peace offering, but a perfection or completion offering. The resurrection brings spirit, soul, and body back together to complete them.

(continued)	Significantly, a *shlamim* offering must be completely eaten within three days. One who eats on the third day is offensive, and the one who keeps eating is considered guilty![349] The penalty is to be "cut off from his kin."[350]
A fire, continually, will remain aflame on the Mizbe'ach; you shall not extinguish it.	"Blessed and holy is the one who has a part in the first resurrection; over these the second death has no power, but they will be priests of God and of Christ and will reign with Him for a thousand years." (Re 20:6) Those who enter into the first resurrection are eternally aflame like the One who has eyes like a "flame of fire," for he was the resurrection offering, and the righteous have followed him by offering themselves for the Kingdom as well.

Hidden North

Another requirement for the olah offering is that it was to be slaughtered on the north (*tzafunah*) side of the altar (Le 1:11). This is the "hidden" side, for *tzafon* in Hebrew can also mean hidden. Could the location of Yeshua's crucifixion tree have been located north of the altar? The slaughter of the purification offering for a priest also was the north side of the altar. In these types, both the resurrected person and the priesthood is symbolically slain north of the altar, or "hidden." This describes the location of the souls "under" the altar in Revelation, resting and hidden from the rest of their people on earth for "a little while."

349. Le. 7:18; 19:5-8

350. The Hebrew word translated as "kin" is "people." The resurrection will include all one's "people," or those within the Body of Messiah.

227

Great is the LORD, and greatly to be praised, in the city of our God, His holy mountain. Beautiful in elevation, the joy of the whole earth, is Mount Zion in the far [sides] north, the city of the great King. God, in her palaces, has made Himself known as a stronghold.[351]

If one wonders how large the Lower Garden or Palace of Messiah is, it could only be speculation, for it is a spiritual realm already present, "at hand." Unlike Yeshua, believers today cannot yet move at will between the physical earth and the spiritual Kingdom, nor can they "time travel" like Yeshua or his disciple Philip when he went into the Ethiopian's chariot to explain the scroll of Isaiah. Without supernatural intervention, one either is alive on earth or she "enters in" the Lower Garden. Some of the prophets, and perhaps Mary in the Garden, briefly "entered in." Elijah and Enoch possibly can move at will between the two realms.

If the Cave of Machpelah in Hebron is the location of the "entrance" to the Garden, and Mount Zion in Jerusalem is the north side of the altar, as well as north from Hebron, then even the literal territory spans quite a distance. It is over 17 miles from Jerusalem to Hebron. The town of Efrat[352] (or "Ephratah," adjacent to Bethlehem) is halfway between Hebron and Jerusalem, and Rachel is buried on the road to Efrat/Bethlehem.

Efrat also means "fruitfulness," denoting the Feast of Tabernacles, yet astoundingly, it also means "ash-heap"! The olah resurrection appears again! From the ash-heap of righteous souls come the resurrected bodies who cross the fruitful Burning River to the Throne. In fact, the flames from the olah offering are considered by mystics to be in the form of a lion,[353] which intersects Micah's prophecy to Efrat, who is "little among Judah." Efrat may be

351. Ps 48:1-3

352. "But thou, Bethlehem Ephratah, though thou be little among the thousands of Judah, yet out of thee shall he come forth unto me that is to be ruler in Israel; whose goings forth have been from of old, from everlasting." (Mi 5:2 KJV)

353. SECTION 40 - RIVER OF FIRE - NAHAR DINUR. http://www. yeshshem.com/ zohar-vayikra-section-40.htm

little or "hidden," yet from her holocaust of innocents emerged the Lion of Judah who is a consuming fire from the Throne.

There is another offering clue in Leviticus, the description of the meal offering. A token portion of the offering is removed and burned on the altar, and then the remainder is baked into unleavened bread, or matzah. This offering was considered like the purification offering of the priests, and it was only for the priesthood to eat.

Unleavened bread accompanied the Hebrews in their exodus from Egypt, and each year it is eaten for seven days in remembrance of the Passover. As the Hebrews fled with their unleavened bread, however, they realized that they were pinned against the sea:

> Then the Egyptians chased after
> them with all the horses and chariots
> of Pharaoh, his horsemen and his
> army, and they overtook them
> camping by the sea, beside Pi-
> hahiroth, *in front* of *Baal-zephon*[354]

The place-name Baal-zephon is a hint, for it means "Lord of the North." While it likely alluded to an Egyptian god or an honorary name for Pharaoh, there is a true Lord of the North, the God of Abraham, Isaac, and Jacob. He rescued the Israelites from Pharaoh, mastering every Egyptian god and Pharaoh himself. The Israelites camped in front of the Lord of the North. The Israelites cried out to Moses: "Is it because there were no graves in Egypt that you have taken us away to die in the wilderness?"

Well, yes, actually Moses did bring them to die in wilderness graves. A tribulation in Hebrew is a tight, narrow place where there is no room to turn around. It constricts one's movements. Even the word Egypt denotes tribulation. In Hebrew, Egypt is *Mitzraim*, or "from tribulations."

354. Ex 14:2, 9

The Holy One of Israel brought the Hebrews from one tribulation, serving Pharaoh, to another, being trapped between Pharaoh's army behind and the Lord of the North before them. Facing one's worst fear is a type of death, such as Abraham offering his only son as an olah. Nevertheless, the olah is a type of grave for resurrection. It burns up everything inside, leaving only the skin!

> The angel of God, who had been going *before the camp* of Israel, moved and went behind them; and the pillar of cloud moved from *before them* and stood behind them.[355]

Both the angel of God and pillar of cloud moved from before the camp and went behind them to guard them during the night. So was Baal-zephon a name-place, or a characteristic of the angel of God, who was first before them, then he moved to block Pharaoh's army? "Baal" in Hebrew doesn't just mean god or master, it means husband. The wordplay implies that the Hidden Husband both led and protected the Israelites through their death and resurrection.

While the Egyptians believe that the Israelites are hopelessly trapped, the Hidden Husband, or Lord of the North, takes the opportunity to send salvation by way of the hot, burning east wind that blew all night,[356] hiding the miracle like the evening olah that burns until morning. In the morning is another olah, the crossing of the sea, a type of immersion to life. The waters part for the Hebrews, but the unseen hand sweeps them back over the Egyptians at daybreak.

In Jewish tradition, there is a crossing of rivers after death.[357] First, the departed soul crosses the River of Light (*Nahar Dinur*)[358] to enter the Lower Garden. Once again, one crosses and immerses in the Burning River from the Lower to the Upper Garden after

355. Ex 14:19

356. Ex 14:21

357. Raphael, p. 309

358. The earliest mention of the River of Fire is in the Book of Daniel where it is described as a Throne of "fiery flames, and wheels of burning fire" (Daniel 7:9). Daniel sees a *nahar dinur*: "A river of fire issued and came forth from before Him; with thousands upon thousands ministering unto Him, and ten thousand upon ten thousand standing before him."

one is completely purified and taught in the Lower Garden. The hint is found in the Genesis Two list of the Rivers of Eden.[359] The very definition of a river (*nahar*) in Hebrew is something burning and shining.

Which river is the Burning River into which one immerses before ascending? An educated guess is the Perat River, called the Euphrates in the earthly realm. In Hebrew, Perat means fruitful. In Genesis 2, it was the river that ran out of (Upper Eden) and watered the whole (Lower) Garden of Eden, supplying the other three rivers that circled the Garden. Or perhaps the initial immersion into the River of Light is the Pishon, or the outer river circling the Garden. Its natural counterpart is thought to be the Nile River, for it was beside its banks that the *pishton*, or the flax, for the linen garments grew. Again, this is speculation, but the clues point back to the Garden.

359. See *Creation Gospel Workbook One Volume 1* for a comprehensive study of the Rivers of Eden.

21

RIVERS OF LIVING WATER

The Biblical prophetess Miriam's life teaches about the rivers of Eden and the hope of resurrection. Miriam watched over her baby brother Moses in the Nile, which is the natural river that represents the outermost river of the Lower Garden, the Pishon. Although Miriam knows that every other Hebrew boy who has been thrown into the Nile by the Egyptians has died, she has faith that the God of Israel can rescue him, so she waits. In fact, Adonai does so through the hand of Pharaoh's daughter, who, like Miriam, is said to be one of the Torah teachers in the Lower Garden.

As Rabbi Fohrman points out,[360] in this instance at the Nile where Moses' life is threatened, Miriam "stands still and sees the salvation of the Lord." It is an act of faith standing among the reeds of the Nile.

Later, the whole nation of Israel is threatened by an entire Egyptian army at the Reed Sea,[361] a whole sea full of reeds. Miriam had already led by example in faith, and Moses tells the Israelites to stand still and see the Salvation of the Lord. In ancient times, reeds were used as writing and measuring instruments. Miriam hints that Israel should have faith in the Word, and every person receives a certain measure of

360. "Why Did Moses Hit the Rock?"

361. "Red Sea" is a mistranslation of *Yam Suf*, or Reed Sea.

faith that can be exercised in it. All you have to do is stand and watch!

If we extend Miriam's stand as a prophecy of hope in resurrection, the layers of faith become deeper. She believed that Moses could be resurrected from the River just as Abraham believed Isaac could be resurrected from the altar. She was the pattern by which Israel was exhorted to believe in their resurrection from the Sea of Reeds, a journey that would kill those who pursued them with chariots and horses. Moses stood before them because of Miriam's faith in the resurrection, so they, too, could believe in a resurrection of water.

"Some trust in chariots, and some in horses, but we will remember the Name of the LORD our God,"[362] is a psalm of contrasting belief in the power of one's own strength, which is perishable and lacks faith in the One who created everything. It is contrasted with faith in the Name of God, which is imperishable, and it is the strength of resurrection. Psalm 20:8 goes on to establish this hope: "They [who hope in chariots and horses] are brought down and fallen: but we are *risen*, and stand upright."

When the people cry out for water three days after crossing the Reed Sea, Moses solves the crisis by taking a stick of wood and throwing it into bitter water to sweeten it. This three-day water hint is another one to the resurrection. To the wicked, the water is undrinkable, unsurvivable. To the one with faith, the water imparts life for the journey.

Miriam's faith lesson saves Moses' life once again at the next water crisis, for the people wanted to stone him. This is the time that Moses is told to strike the rock, and this is the rock that becomes "Miriam's Well."

362. Ps 20:7; Is 31:1

Take Miriam's name; Mem, Reish, Yud, Mem. Remove all vowelization, so you just have Mem, Reish, Yud, Mem...if you vowelize Mem, Reish, Yud, Mem one way it can mean Marim - bitter. If you vowelize it another way it can mean; Meirim - to lift up. If you vowelize it yet another way it can mean; Morim - rebels. Now think about these words, where did they show up? Water crisis number 1, how come they couldn't drink the water? Ki marim heim - the waters were bitter. There's Marim - Mem, Reish, Yud, Mem. Water crisis number 3, right before Moses hits the rock he lifts up his hand; Vayarem - that comes from Meirim - to lift up. Finally, when he speaks to the people in concert with hitting the rock; Shimu nah hamorim, he says - listen you rebels, Mem, Reish, Yud, Mem once again.

Every, single possible permutation of Miriam's name shows up in the water crises, in which the first one Miriam sings, the last one she dies, in the middle one her rock becomes this well, Miriam is everywhere in these water crises stories...[363]

John has a vision of a New Jerusalem "coming down." One may assume to the natural earth, but what if he means from the Upper Garden to the Lower Garden like the River of Upper Eden that watered the whole Lower Garden?

> And he shewed me a pure river
> of water of life, clear as crystal,
> proceeding out of the throne of God
> and of the Lamb.[364]

The Perat, or fruitful river, connotes the Feast of Sukkot

363. Fohrman

364. Re 22:1

(Tabernacles), which included offerings of every kind of fruit and produce. It was Sukkot in which the Jews practiced the water-pouring ceremony accompanied by wine-pouring.

According to Jewish tradition, the four rivers of Eden are honey, wine, balsam, and milk.[365] Yeshua stood at the Feast of Sukkot water-pouring ceremony and proclaimed himself to be that River of eternal life. He connects the resting souls of the Lower Garden with the Upper Garden. When New Jerusalem descends in Revelation 22, John describes twelve types of fruit that grow along the River, and the leaves heal the nations. This is consistent with rabbinic tradition.

Remarkably, the tree grows on both sides of the River, and although it is only one tree, it bears twelve types of fruit:

365. Song of Solomon 5:1

366. Re 22:1-2

367. "He sent His word and healed them, and delivered them from their destructions." (Ps 107:20); "Lord, I am not worthy for You to come under my roof, but just say the **word**, and my servant will be **healed**. (Mt 8:8) "When evening came, they brought to Him many who were demon-possessed, and He cast out the spirits with a word and healed all who were ill." (Mt. 8:16)

> Then he showed me a river of the water of life, clear as crystal, coming from the throne of God and of the Lamb, in the middle of its street. On either side of the river was the tree of life, bearing twelve kinds of fruit, yielding its fruit every month; and the leaves of the tree were for the healing of the nations.[366]

The Tree of Life is a metaphor for the Torah, the Word of God. As in the Garden of Eden, the Tree is associated with a river. Water is a metaphor for the Torah just as the Tree of Life, and in Revelation 22:1-2, it is associated with its healing qualities.[367]

> Water, in general, had other metaphoric meanings that many Jews would have appreciated. Selkin has analyzed rabbinic traditions identifying water with Torah and has demonstrated how the words of Torah were regarded as a

236

'purifying pool' for Israel.'[368]

As a result, in the early centuries, some Jewish sects would immerse in water before Torah study or prayer, for it was thought to renew their minds for study and to prepare for the Presence of the Holy Spirit invited by mindful prayer and study.

As John mentioned in Chapter 22, there is no need for the physical light of the sun and moon in the Holy City of the World to Come because the light source is The Holy One. The descending upper city is one in which there is no more death and the "first things" are passed away. This suggests that the full descent of the righteous in the New Jerusalem occurs after the judgment of the "books," which occurs at the second resurrection.

> And I saw the holy city, new Jerusalem, coming down out of heaven from God, made ready as a bride adorned for her husband. And I heard a loud voice from the throne, saying, 'Behold, the tabernacle of God is among men, and He will dwell among them, and they shall be His people, and God Himself will be among them, and He will wipe away every tear from their eyes; and there will no longer be any death; there will no longer be any mourning, or crying, or pain; the first things have passed away.' (Re 21:2-4) "...Then one of the seven angels who had the seven bowls full of the seven last plagues came and spoke with me, saying, 'Come here, I will show you the bride, the wife of the Lamb." (21:9)

The New Jerusalem's inauguration as the permanent residence of the righteous after the second

368. Miller, 2007, p. 224

resurrection is accompanied by the disposal of the wicked souls in the "lake that burns with fire," which is known as the second death:

> He who overcomes will inherit these things, and I will be his God and he will be My son. But for the cowardly and unbelieving and abominable and murderers and immoral persons and sorcerers and idolaters and all liars, their part will be in the lake that burns with fire and brimstone, which is the second death."[369]

Can a soul die twice?

Apparently, yes. The unrepentant wicked would never survive the trip across the River of Light, for it is holy and for the sustenance of the holy ones.[370] The "lake of fire" is an apt description of the abode of the wicked who will likely be bundled together similarly to the way the Body of Messiah is bundled together in the "bundle of the living."[371]

Can a soul resurrect twice?

Perhaps. If it is a matter of an even greater spiritual transformation to enter the gates of the Upper Garden when the books open at the second resurrection, maybe so. A clue is in the following verse (9):

> Come here, I will show you the bride, the wife of the Lamb.

369. Re 21:7-8

370. Singh, 1926. Expanded text found in Appendix B.

371. 1 Sa 25:29

The "bride adorned for her husband," the wife of the Lamb, may be able to go from a Lower Garden, according to the Apostle Paul, which is already unspeakable to human understanding, to a Garden City home for the virtuous Wife of the Hidden Husband. The Throne of this city issues a fruitful river of Sukkot, yet Sukkot is the last feast of the Biblical year, and Passover is the first. To the understanding student, the chiasm is apparent. That which was hidden at Passover openly gives life at Sukkot!

Both the angels in the empty tomb and the Gardener ask Mary, "Woman [Ishah], why are you weeping?" The maror and salt water of each Passover meal represent the bitterness of slavery and the bitter tears shed in Egypt, but may they also represent the bitter tears shed by Sarah for resurrection at the entrance to the Garden and the tears that will be forever wiped away at the second resurrection?

The importance of Yeshua calling Miriam Ishah, or Woman, Wife, cannot be overstated. She was the first human to testify of the resurrection, which is the behavior befitting those who have "the testimony of Yeshua and the commandments of God." She was the first living righteous human being to see the resurrection of the Hidden Husband. He would be hidden again when he ascended to the Father, but for a moment, Miriam stood in the Garden with the Tree of Life.

Every year a piece of matzah[372] is wrapped in a linen napkin and hidden during the Passover; this is called the tzafun. Tzafun means locked away, hidden, buried, and out of reach, like Baal-tzaphon. A rescue from tribulation is found in the hidden salvation (yeshuat) of Yeshua, who was wrapped in linen and hidden in a tomb at Passover. That burned token portion was resurrected from the purifying meal-offering fire, and eating that unleavened bread of truth purifies a nation of hidden and buried priests preparing for resurrection today.

Jewish mystics also see the tzafun as representing the hidden life force of the soul. "If the soul is light, then that essence is the source of light."[373] As the soul awaits the first resurrection in the Lower Garden, that hidden life force is further purified, ever burnishing the

372. unleavened bread

373. "Tzafun-Eat the Afikomen."

light from within. At the resurrection, the Husband, no longer hidden, will unite all the righteous and shining hidden priests into a glowing resurrection cloud. How much more would they shine at a second resurrection?

22

SONG OF SONGS FOR PASSOVER

Each year, Jews read the Song of Songs at the time of Passover. Like the Passover, it is the story of Israel and her resurrection. Knowing some of the Biblical symbols discussed in this book as well as some of the Jewish ideas about life, death, and resurrection, verses can now come alive with greater meaning. Let's take a few verses to practice "stringing pearls," or connecting the same idea in different parts of Scripture.

> How beautiful is your love, my sister,
> my bride! How much better is your
> love than wine, and the fragrance of
> your oils. Than all kinds of spices![374]

In Proverbs, the sister is a metaphor of the Spirit of Wisdom, the first of the Seven Spirits of Adonai listed in Isaiah. This double-entendre is used by Abraham and Isaac when they tell Sarah and Rebekah, "Say you're my sister" to save their lives from a wicked Pharaoh and a wicked king, Abimelech. It is more than just saving their skins, prophetically, they speak of the Holy Spirit as a Helper. In this sense, the bride is a sister, too. As an example, in Revelation, "The Spirit and the Bride say, 'Come." So which is it? Yes. If the Spirit is in the Bride, then she says, "Come."

374. Sng 4:10

A garden locked is my sister, my
bride, a rock garden locked, a spring
sealed up.[375]

I have come into my garden, my
sister, my bride; I have gathered
my myrrh along with my balsam. I
have eaten my honeycomb and my
honey; I have drunk my wine and my
milk. Eat, friends; Drink and imbibe
deeply, O lovers."[376]

The song references the sister/bride as a garden, a
sealed-up spring. It denotes modesty and protection
of what is in the garden. Inside the garden are the
balsam, honey, wine, and milk said to flow in the
Rivers of Eden.

I was asleep but my heart was
awake. A voice! My beloved was
knocking: 'Open to me, my sister,
my darling, my dove, my perfect
one! For my head is drenched with
dew, my locks with the damp of the
night.'[377]

Although the writer is "asleep," a metaphor of
death, her heart is awake, so she hears the sound
of Yeshua knocking. The beloved is also called a
"dove, my perfect one." The height of Gan Eden
is said to be no higher than the height a dove can
fly, and its palace is the Bird's Nest. A dove denotes
a resting place, as in Noah's dove of a resurrected
earth. The head drenched with early morning dew is
a metaphor of resurrection, which is associated with
dew of Heaven. It was early in the morning when
Miriam encountered the resurrected Yeshua:

375. Sng 4:12

376. Sng 5:1

377. Sng 5:2

Now on the first day of the week
Mary Magdalene came early to the
tomb, while it was still dark, and saw
the stone already taken away from

the tomb.[378]

> Your dead will live; their corpses will
> rise. You who lie in the dust, awake
> and shout for joy, for your dew is
> as the dew of the dawn, and the
> earth will give birth to the departed
> spirits.[379]

The dove can represent approval and praiseworthiness.

> But my dove, my perfect one, is
> unique: She is her mother's only
> daughter; she is the pure child of
> the one who bore her. The maidens
> saw her and called her blessed, the
> queens and the concubines also,
> and they praised her...[380]

One precedent for this is the event following Yeshua's immersion in water. The Father immediately gives His approval to His beloved son in whom He is well-pleased. The heavens opened, and the Spirit descended "like a dove":

> Immediately coming up out of the
> water, He saw the heavens opening,
> and the Spirit like a dove descending
> upon Him...[381]

Now the Jewish tradition of the Garden of Eden being no higher than a dove can fly makes sense. Truly, the Kingdom of Heaven is at hand.

378. Jn 20:1

379. Is 26:19

380. Sng 6:9

381. Mk 1:10

23

CONCLUSION

Yeshua preached, taught, and evangelized repetitively and passionately about the Kingdom of Heaven. He did not teach in starry-eyed homilies of some far-off utopia. Yeshua taught about a Kingdom that is "at hand." You can actually touch it within the span of your life even if you can only enter it after death to fully enjoy its higher levels after the resurrection. What can distinguish a disciple of Yeshua is how he or she engages in this life. A life marked by the "fear of Heaven," or a consciousness of the nearness of the Kingdom, urges the individual to fine-tune mere natural hearing to spiritual hearing.

Spiritual hearing is available as the Ruach HaKodesh (Holy Spirit) writes the Word on the hearts of believers. That Word will change priorities for those who seek that unseen Kingdom that is so close. The activities, study, and beliefs that one practices in this life follow into the Kingdom. The more one attaches to the Kingdom things, the less the opportunity for attachment to things that vaporize upon death or at the return of Messiah at the resurrection. The more one is attached to Kingdom things, the less the pain of leaving the only home the soul has ever known, the body.

Although this booklet is not to be internalized as doctrine, but food for study, comparison, and thought concerning death and resurrection, one principle seems only common sense: a little bit of tribulation now to discipline one's thoughts and desires toward the Kingdom, the less tribulation of the soul when it realizes that its home is no longer the physical body. A soul excessively attached to the treasures of ballgames, videogames, social media, long vacations, hunting and fishing, movies, one's secular work, or religious deeds performed to be noticed by others, will have difficulty attaching to the Lower Garden. It may be a painful, instead of a natural, separation, explaining why souls are thought to hover around their corpses for a few days, for the separation of death is an experience of emotional upheaval for the wicked or intermediate.[382]

Upon death, one will still be what one was in mortality, but in the Garden, non-Kingdom priorities gradually fade from consciousness. For instance, when this author retired from a career in law enforcement, the feeling of being a law enforcement officer lingered. After a few years passed, that mindfulness in thought and identity faded. That being is still there, but the things that were so important in daily work are rarely brought to mind anymore unless something provokes it. So it will be with this mortal life and activities that vaporize upon death. The illusion is that these things were really living; the truth is they add nothing to one's eternal identity and existence.

382. Some sources say that one class of unclean spirits are dead who flee the sequence of post-mortem experiences, and they flit around until forced into Sheol by angels tasked with that job. Allegedly, they will attempt to attach to people or animals in order to remain on earth.

What feels good to the soul today may be a source of anguish and regret at that unknown moment of death. By settling for lower places of self-gratification, we unwittingly lower the bar of our existence in a place so wonderful that even Paul couldn't describe it. If we limit our spiritual life in the Lower Garden, how much more would that limit our access to holier places in the Upper Garden?

The higher heavens is a topic best kept for another

time. If the Apostle Paul was not permitted to speak of the things he heard in the Lower Garden, then who are we to presume that we can competently speculate of that which is higher above? What we can do, however, is carefully examine every statement and parable that Yeshua taught concerning the Kingdom. They are not platitudes, but practical, serious advice on the choices we make today, this moment, and every moment. We can study the Torah, Prophets, and Psalms for more clues about what is to come, but what really matters is if it changes today.

Every moment, we prepare for our Garden.

What about our loved ones who have gone before? The thief on the cross gives us hope that even the rascals can call out a moment before death. They may not have the same Garden experience as those who have suffered greatly for their faith, but Yeshua said the Father's House has many chambers. Preparation is happening even now.

For our loved ones who lived lives of faith, then they have entered into the Father's joy in the Garden. They are waiting for you. They are conscious of you. They, too, are likely very busy about the Father's business, learning and preparing for greater delights to come. Let's use an earthly example of when we, too, will cross over and enter the Garden if Yeshua's return is delayed.

When we pass, those who love us on earth will be saying their farewells while we enter the Arrivals hall in the Garden. Go to an airport and watch the greetings, smiles, and joy, when a long-lost relative or soldier descends the escalator, looking around, maybe a little afraid that no one will be there. Then he sees his family and friends waiting, cheering, waving, jumping, singing, and holding their arms out for a first hug. The family dog is wearing a "Welcome Home" bandana and barking. That's when the passenger realizes the crowd is all there to greet him. He's the one they've been waiting for.

Multiply that scene by the number of all your righteous family and ancestors. When you *ascend*, they'll all...along with a few other dignitaries...be waiting expectantly.

Welcome home, good and faithful servant. We've been waiting for you.

REFERENCES

Angel, M. (2000). *Exploring Sephardic customs and traditions.* Brooklyn, NY: Ktav Publishing House.

Appel, G. & Goldstein, D. (2016). *Concise code of Jewish law: a guide to the observance of   Shabbat.* New York: OU Press.

Bar Tzadok, A. (1993). *Aliens, angels, and demons.* Tellico Plains, TN: The Kosher Torah School.

Berliner, Ed. (1591). *Targum pseudo-Jonathan.* Venice. Sabbionetta.

_____. (1557). *Targum Onkelos.* Sabbionetta.

Biderman, A. (2011). *The Mishkan – the Tabernacle: Its structure and its sacred vessels.* New York: Mesorah Publications, Ltd.

Bohrer, Y. (2007). *The geographic codes of the Bible.* Israel: Studio Bat Ami, Bet-El.

Dalman, G & Lightfoot, J. (2002). *Jesus Christ in the Talmud and commentary on the Gospels from the Talmud and the Hebraica.* (R. Parrish, Ed.). Eugene, OR: Resource Publications.

Drazin, I. (2000). *Targum Onkelos.* Denver: Ktav Publishing House, Inc.

Eastman, M. (1897). *Eastman's Bible dictionary.* New York: Thomas Nelson.

Fohrman, D. Chukkat: "Why Did Moses Hit the Rock?" alphabeta. org, retrieved 7-13-18.

Ganor, Y & Ganor, O. "Chukkat." Ulpan Or e-newsletter. Retrieved 6/22/18. Jerusalem: Israel. https://www.ulpanor.com/category/newletter/

Gillman, N. (2015). *The death of death: resurrection and immortality in Jewish thought.* Woodstock, VT: Jewish Lights Publishing.

Kahn, A. (2012). *Echoes of Eden: Sefer Shemot.* Jerusalem, Israel: Gefen Publishing House.

_____. (2002). *Emanations.* Southfield, MI: Targum Press.

Kaplan, A. (1993). *Immortality, resurrection, and the age of the universe.* New York: Association of Orthodox Jewish Scientists

Lieber, D., (Ed). *Etz Chaim Torah and commentary.* (2001). New York: Jewish Publication Society.

Lichtman, M. (2006). *Eretz Yisrael in the parasha.* Jerusalem, Israel: Devorah Publishing.

Luzatto, M. (2007). *The complete messilat yesharim.* Jerusalem: Ofeq Institute

Miller, S. (2007). "Stepped Pools and the Non-Existent Monolithic 'Miqveh.'" Edwards, D. & McCollough, T., Eds., *The archaeology of difference: gender, ethnicity, class and the 'other' in antiquity.* Vol. 60/61.

Nemoy, L., Lieberman, S., et al, Eds, (1968). *Pesikta Rabbati: Homiletical discourses for festal days and special Sabbaths 1 & 2.* Braude, G., Trans., New York: Yale University Press.

Raphael, S. (2009). *Jewish views of the afterlife.* 2d Ed. New York: Rowman and Littlefield Publishers, Inc.

Scherman, N. & Zlotowitz, M., Eds. (1997). *The Torah: With Rashi's commentary translated, annotated, and elucidated.* Sapirstein Ed. New York: Mesorah Publications, Ltd.

Riskin, S. "Ohr Torah on the parsha: 'Why was Sarah in Hevron?'" *Israel National News.* 11/6/15 Retrieved from http://www.israelnationalnews.com/Articles/Article.aspx/17845.

Salanter, Y. (2004). *Ohr Yisrael.* Zvi Miller, Trans. Southfield, MI:

Targum Press, Inc.

Saldarini, A. (2001). *Pharisees, scribes, and Sadducees in Palestinian society: a sociological approach.* (electronic ed.). Grand Rapids, MI: Eerdmans.

Scherman, N., Ed. (1996). *The complete artscroll siddur.* Nusach Sefard. New York: Mesorah Publications, Ltd.

"Section of Ancient Jerusalem Aqueduct Uncovered." By TOI STAFF. 21 May 2015. *The Times of Israel.* https://www.timesofisrael. com/section-of-ancient-jerusalem-aqueduct-   uncovered/

Singh, S. (1926). *The visions of Sadhu Sundar Singh of India.* Armidale, Australia: Noah's Ark. 1996.

Sperber, A. (1959). *The Bible in Aramaic* Netherlands: E. J. Brill.

Strassfeld, M. (1985). *The Jewish holidays: a guide and commentary.* New York: Harper Collins.

"Tzafun-Eat the Afikomen." Chabad.org. Retrieved 3/24/18. https://www.chabad.org/holidays/passover/pesach_cdo/ aid/117123/jewish/12-Tzafun-Eat-the-Afikoman.htm.

Utley, R. (2003). Luke the historian: The book of Acts (Vol. 3B). *Study Guide Commentary Series* Marshall, TX: Bible Lessons International.

Yerushalmi, M. (2007). *From Baghdad to Jerusalem.* E. Yerushalmi & D. Yerushalmi, Trans. Tel Aviv: Kotarot Publishing. Originally published as *The Journey of Abu-Moch.*

Zalman, S., (Ed). (2003). *Machzor for Rosh HaShanah.* Mangel, N., Trans., New York: Merkos L'Inyonei Chinuch

APPENDIX A

Menorah with Creation, Seven Spirits, Seven Feasts, and Seven Assemblies of Revelation

APPENDIX B

Chiastic Cut-out

ABOUT THE
AUTHOR

Dr. Hollisa Alewine has her B.S. and M.Ed. from Texas A&M and a Doctorate from Oxford Graduate School; she is the author of Standing with Israel: A House of Prayer for All Nations, The Creation Gospel Bible study series, and a programmer on Hebraic Roots Network. Dr. Alewine is a student and teacher of the Word of God.

Made in the USA
San Bernardino,
CA